what others are saying

"Lacy has the provocative ability to blend the Sacred and the practical, the spiritual and the everyday, in wisdom-full and passionate ways. In *Pilgrim Principles*, she takes you by the hand (and heart), gently guiding you with prose, prayer, and praxis; inviting and compelling meaningful ways of integrating faith, hope, and love with the everyday stuff of life. You can trust her. Buy the book. Take the journey."

Ronna Detrick, MDiv
ronnadetrick.com

"Lacy weaves classic pilgrimage wisdom with fresh, accessible insight. She skillfully includes uncommon words like *quotidian* alongside her own creative *Pilgrim Glasses*, reminding us to see the Sacred in everything. This book is the perfect pilgrim's pack—filled with essentials, necessities, and a touch of surprise!"

Kayce S. Hughlett
author of As I Lay Pondering: Daily Invitations
to Live a Transformed Life
kaycehughlett.com

"Through her practical, invitational, and inspirational *Pilgrim Principles*, Lacy provides holistic guidance to experience daily life as an earthly pilgrimage. This book is a field guide for the pilgrim's soul and a sacred tool for transformation for those seeking ways to enrich their inner and outer journeys."

Sybil Dana Reynolds
Spiritual Director, author of Ink and Honey
sacredlifearts.com

"Lacy takes you on a journey you've always longed for but never knew how to begin. With her as your gracious and eloquent guide, you'll find yourself asking questions that move your soul and lead to meaningful discoveries. But beware, this is no quick read of quips and cliché advice. Pack your bags and bring along a few extra journals. The challenges and exercises will take you through meditation, practice, and reflection—all fueled by a hope that you will know your creator, your world, and yourself far better than before."

Victor Saad
founder of The Experience Institute
author of The Leap Year Project

"Like an archaeologist preparing a precious lost artifact for display, Lacy brings the ancient art of pilgrimage into the spotlight of our modern world with great care and delight. *Pilgrim Principles* is a gentle call to the Sacred in all of our daily journeys—a reminder that we are travelers in this world whether we leave home or not—and the opportunity to traverse this life with intention is one we can't afford not to take. Lacy is a qualified and generous guide in this journey, one that brings readers closer to their true selves by the end."

Abby Hollingsworth
dearabbyleigh.com

"Lacy is a woman of great depth and insight. Her work and words continually call me into deeper places of meaning and authenticity. Listen closely to what she has to say! She will take you to surprising and important places—personally, emotionally, spiritually, and physically."

Dan Cumberland
themeaningmovement.com

PILGRIM PRINCIPLES

*journeying with intention
in everyday life*

A SEVEN WEEK JOURNEY RIGHT AT HOME

LACY CLARK ELLMAN

*Foreword by Christine Valters Paintner, PhD
Online Abbess at AbbeyoftheArts.com*

Book design: Modern Etiquette Design (modernetiquettedesign.com)
Cover and author images: Sparkfly Photography (sparkflyphotography.com)

ISBN: 978-1494306243

To my younger self (and those who also search)—
I know why you wander, and what you seek is good.

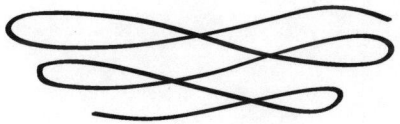

CONTENTS

CONTENTS

FOREWORD

Ideally, a human life should be a constant pilgrimage of discovery. The most exciting discoveries happen at the frontiers. When you come to know something new, you come closer to yourself and to the world. Discovery enlarges and refines your sensibility. When you discover something, you transfigure some of the forsakenness of the world.

—John O'Donohue, *Eternal Echoes: Celtic Reflections on Our Yearning to Belong*

THE SCRIPTURES ARE FILLED with journeys: Abraham called away from the land which was familiar, Moses leading the Israelites out of slavery in Egypt, the Prodigal Son leaving home and returning to a father's welcome, Mary and Joseph seeking a place to give birth, Jesus' wandering and final journey to Jerusalem, the encounter on the road to Emmaus, even the story of Adam and Eve is a journey from Paradise out into the world.

Journeys are movements from one place to another, often to a place that is unfamiliar, foreign, and strange. A pilgrimage is an intentional journey into this experience of unknowing and discomfort for the sake of stripping away preconceived ideas and expectations and growing closer to the God beyond our own imagination. In recent years there has been a great reclaiming of the practice of pilgrimage, which flourished in the Middle Ages. More than ever, we feel called to walk in holy places and make new discoveries.

In the spring of 2012 my husband and I embarked on our own great journey and pilgrimage. We experienced a call to sell everything we owned—home, car, furniture, books, and other belongings—and board a ship crossing the Atlantic ocean. For several years prior we had been making smaller pilgrimages to Europe, seeking out ancestral places like Ireland and England, the land of our mothers' ancestors, and Germany and Austria, the land of our fathers' ancestors. Now we live in Ireland and continue to discover what this journey is about.

I believe very much in taking physical pilgrimages to faraway places. I know the value of stepping into foreign cultures and illuminating all the expectations I hold about how life should work. But I also believe that pilgrimage is very much an inner journey and experience. There are those who can travel long distances, but never see the place they visit except through the lens of a tourist. And there are those who may not travel very far on an outward path, but the inward distance is long and arduous. We can cultivate the soul of a pilgrim when we stay open to a way of life that is always open to newness.

I first met Lacy Clark Ellman when she was finishing her graduate studies and attended a training I was leading. I was delighted by her passion and to learn of her own love of pilgrimage and have witnessed the beautiful growth of her work in this area, inviting people into precisely this experience of inner pilgrimage through reflections on her website. She is building a community of people longing for their own experience of discovery.

Lacy offers us a gift in this book, the invitation to make our own inner journey through practices of ancient wisdom. While ultimately pilgrimage demands that we let go of maps and listen to an inner compass, Lacy provides a guide of sorts to the rigorous and rewarding challenges of navigating the soul's landscape.

Blessings on the journey ahead,

Christine Valters Paintner, PhD
Online Abbess at AbbeyoftheArts.com

INTRODUCTION

My Own Journey (and yours, too)

I HAVE BEEN A TRAVELER for as long as I can remember. Whether by plane or a good old-fashioned road trip, I have spent a lot of my life traveling to diverse places and discovering new cultures. I took my first trip abroad with my mother and grandmother when I was eight. We spent over a week in London and the surrounding area, where my world was opened to different sights, unfamiliar sounds, and new experiences. (Take toast racks, for example. I love how they lend such refined presentation to a simple breakfast.)

As I grew older, I continued to travel, both in the United States and abroad. My deep affection for seeing the world was solidified, however, on my first trip to Europe without my family. As I journeyed on whim from place to place after my first year of college, my pack on my back and my passport in hand, a seed was planted: my passion for travel. This seed was watered soon after with a semester abroad in London, more traveling throughout Eastern Europe, and a gap year spent in the "Jewel of Africa": Uganda.

While my passion for travel continued to grow, another seed was taking root within me and wouldn't let go: my yearning for God.

As I continued to travel to places beyond my borders, experiencing things different from my day-to-day, my spirituality began to stretch as well. I began to sense the presence of God in new ways and grew hungry for spiritual encounter. I yearned to encounter God in everything, most of all when I was in the transformative circumstances presented in foreign territory. I found that my journeys continuously informed my spirituality, and my spirituality was in turn impacting my journeys. The two seeds that were planted so long ago—my passion for travel and my yearning for God—had grown into resilient and wild vines that were now intertwined.

But the intertwining of spirituality and journeys is not just a reality for me. I believe this is true for all of us. We are all on journeys that take us beyond our borders and inform (and are impacted by) our spirituality. Sometimes our journeys are literal, but we journey in many other ways as well. We journey through careers, relationships, ups and downs, highs and lows. We journey through obstacles and toward accomplishments. We journey through seasons of life and formation. We journey from birth through childhood, adolescence, adulthood, and eventually death. And as we traverse this terrain, we all ask the same essential questions, whether we know it or not:

Who am I?
Who is God?
Where is God?
What is the meaning of life—
In the bigger picture? In the day-to-day?
What makes me come alive?
What do I long for?

These are Sacred questions, and when we ask them with intention and actively engage the search that burns within us, our journeys are transformed.

These Sacred questions that guide us today have been the shared questions of humanity for thousands of years. Throughout history, those who asked these Sacred questions with intention and actively engaged the search that burned within set off on pilgrimages: journeys of Sacred Encounter. These literal journeys brought pilgrims beyond the edge of the day-to-day and into foreign territory that called forth the vulnerability through which Sacred Encounter and transformation often occur.

The practice of pilgrimage is alive and well today, beckoning a new generation of seekers to journey beyond the edge of daily life into terrains of mystery, wonder, revelation, delight, acceptance, and transformation. No matter the itinerary or location, pilgrimage is *a Sacred journey*—a movement that brings us toward the Divine. It is a journey embarked upon with the intention of encountering God and experiencing transformation.

While travel can impact your spirituality in a powerful way, you don't necessarily have to leave home to live like a pilgrim. Pilgrimage speaks to a longing for something more and a faith that something beyond ourselves can be experienced if we are open to the search. To live as a pilgrim at home, all you need to do is see your life as a journey and your role as a seeker of the Sacred.

Journeying with Intention in Everyday Life
(and what you'll find in these pages)

One way you can begin to live as a pilgrim each day is to participate in a *Rule of Life*. A Rule of Life is a set of guidelines to help cultivate meaning in your interior journey, daily routine, and community. Developing and living by a Rule of Life is an ancient tradition practiced by religious communities and individuals alike for centuries. It is not something that these communities and individuals strive to achieve, but rather a basis from which they live.

The book you hold in your hands is based on a Rule of Life I've developed with the pilgrim in mind—*Pilgrim Principles*. Seen through the lens of pilgrimage, this Rule encourages you to maintain the posture of a pilgrim both at home and abroad. This book seeks to immerse you in this Rule of Life and the way of a pilgrim right at home. Each week focuses on a different Pilgrim Principle and includes daily readings, a guided meditation, and ways to engage the principle through practice and reflection. You'll want to have a journal beside you as you read this book, helping you take what you read and incorporate it into your own journey and everyday life.

Some Final Thoughts (and a helpful tool)

This book is setup as seven daily readings over seven weeks—one week for each principle. You can read it as structured or pick it up when the moment seems right. You might find that you've read through an entire week in one sitting! However you decide to read this book, my hope is that you will allow enough time for each reading to sink in and impact you, engaging the practices and letting the reflections stay with you throughout your day. Above all, I hope that this is a resource you can return to again and again whenever you need a reminder that you are not alone on your journey, and that what you most earnestly seek can indeed be found.

A note about the language in what you're about to read: You will notice the word *Sacred* capitalized throughout this book. You'll also see it a lot. When I talk about the Sacred, I'm speaking of God and all things holy and *Divine* (also capitalized, because it's just as significant). I'm talking about all things beautiful, all things tender, and the moments of connection that can both alter your life and warm your soul. You'll notice that I like to refer to the Holy Spirit as the *Sacred Guide*, because it seems so fitting when we look at our lives as a pilgrimage. The *Path of the Pilgrim* is the path that we all share on our Sacred search. And when I talk about moments of *Sacred Encounter*? These are the moments we journey for, whether tiny glimpses of the Divine or experiences that stop us in our paths, filling us with awe. I've included these words and more in a glossary for you to return to as you come across these terms in the readings.

I also speak of the stages of pilgrimage: *departure*, *arrival*, and *return*. These stages come from fellow pilgrim Phil Cousineau and are rooted in the work of the late mythologist Joseph Campbell.[1] In the pilgrim's journey, the stage of departure starts with the pilgrim's search. This search begins the journey, with the pilgrim setting off into the unknown looking for answers and fulfillment. Next comes the stage of arrival. The arrival isn't simply when the pilgrim reaches a destination, but more specifically when the pilgrim encounters the Sacred. These Sacred Encounters leave lasting impact and inspire change. This transition leads the pilgrim into the stage of return, when she re-enters everyday life transformed.

The stages of departure, arrival, and return are a part of all of our journeys, whether at home or abroad. As you learn more about them, you'll likely be able to look back and identify the times of departure, arrival, and return in your own travels or significant seasons of life. It is my hope that this book helps you to do just that. And as you engage the Pilgrim Principles and practices suggested here to guide you in discovering your journeys, I hope that you are also able to make these principles your own.

THE 7 PILGRIM PRINCIPLES

one
A pilgrim looks for the Sacred in the quotidian

two
A pilgrim practices somatic spirituality

three
A pilgrim is a good steward of resources

four
A pilgrim immerses herself in culture

five
A pilgrim creates daily rhythms to ground himself

six
A pilgrim carries herself with curiosity

seven
A pilgrim seeks to know his Inner Witness

A PILGRIM'S GLOSSARY OF TERMS

arrival: The second stage of the pilgrim's journey; includes trials, challenges, and a deep interior quest. The place where the pilgrim's journey and the Divine intersect.

departure: The first stage of the pilgrim's journey; includes the inspiration for and initiation of the journey. As the search begins, the pilgrim transitions to the stage of arrival through impending trials, challenges, and questioning, which bring forth vulnerability and lead to surrender.

Inner Witness: The indwelling of the Holy Spirit; the place within where the true self and the Divine meet.

intention: A purpose or hope; to live and journey with intention is to live and journey with purpose, awareness, and desire.

journey: A storied movement in life and in time resulting in transformation. It is chiefly an interior quest, but can be influenced by exterior passage, as with traditional pilgrimage.

return: The third and final stage of the pilgrim's journey. Because of the events of arrival, a shift occurs and the pilgrim engages life newly transformed.

Sacred and *Divine*: Alternative words for God and all things holy that allow us to explore the mystery that exists beyond our limited understanding. These words also refer to all things beautiful, all things tender, and the moments of connection that can both alter your life and warm your soul.

Sacred Encounter: Moments and circumstances when the true self and the Divine meet in a palpable way that elicits awe and inspires transformation.

Sacred Guide: The Holy Spirit and the ultimate guide on our Sacred journeys.

synchronicity: The uncanny occurrence of the meeting of needs, of the encountering of people, or of things coming together perfectly, making it seem that the stars have aligned to help the pilgrim on her journey.

true self: The whole self as created by God; the essence of your being for which you journey to reveal.

Path of the Pilgrim: The continuous journey of the seeker, both abroad and in everyday life.

pilgrimage: A Sacred journey; a movement toward the Divine. Traditionally a long and treacherous journey to a Sacred site, often taken by foot.

Pilgrim Glasses: When journeys and everyday life are viewed through the lens of pilgrimage.

Pilgrim Principles: A Rule of Life to guide the seeker in practicing pilgrimage every day and engaging journeys with intention.

week one

A PILGRIM LOOKS FOR THE SACRED IN THE QUOTIDIAN

week one: day one

INTRODUCTION

I FIRST CAME ACROSS THE WORD QUOTIDIAN a few years ago in a book called *The Quotidian Mysteries* by Kathleen Norris. The book was recommended to me by a professor in my graduate program with whom I was working to create an independent study course based on daily practices. When I looked it up, I found this:

> quo•tid•i•an [kwo-**tid**-ee-*uh* n], *adjective* [2]
> 1. daily
> 2. usual or customary; everyday
> 3. ordinary; commonplace

In essence, *quotidian* refers to the everyday, ordinary moments that we all face—and must attend to—many times each day: cooking meals, commuting to work, buying groceries, taking care of our families, our bodies, our homes.

You know these moments well, right? Some are like second nature; others feel like perpetual to-dos. And yet, these very moments which are necessary in our lives are fertile ground for Sacred Encounter if we approach them with intention. In fact, that's why I use *quotidian* rather than *ordinary*—because it's not basic; such a strange and beautiful word awakens curiosity and calls us toward something more.

The pilgrim knows this and practices awareness in the ordinary moments each day, delighting in the Divine mysteries and manifestations that surround him, whether it is a bulb sprouting in her garden in the cold days of early spring, the laugh of a loved one at the dinner table, or the face of the homeless person whom she passes on her way home from work. The pilgrim believes all that surrounds him holds significance and can tell him something of the Divine.

It is especially important for the pilgrim to cultivate awareness of the Sacred in the everyday because the journey for the pilgrim is always a journey *toward* the Sacred, whether abroad or in daily life. When finding delight in the Sacred each day, the pilgrim is blessed by and recognizes that which is Sacred, whether in the mind through thanksgiving or with action through engagement.

In this week's readings, we'll explore different moments, elements, and places that are part of our everyday—morning, home, work, community, and night—each offering new ways to look for the Sacred in the quotidian.

REFLECTION

What are some ways you experience the Sacred in your everyday life?

week one: day two

MORNING

THE FIRST PILGRIM PRINCIPLE is all about finding the Sacred in the ordinary—in our ordinary moments, our ordinary encounters, and the ordinary things that surround us daily. Something else that is ordinary and fills our days with their coming and going are our emotions—our feelings, our desires, our fears, and our joys. Some of these emotions can fill our days with darkness, while others can have us whistling a happy tune. Sometimes they come so abruptly that they can have us doing both in a single hour.

Either way, these emotions greet us every morning and are an established part of our day-to-day lives. Some days, the sun gently wakes us, filling us with joy. At other times, the buzzing of the alarm clock on a dark winter's morning can leave us feeling angry and resentful, no matter how sweet our slumber. I know I am often greeted each morning with the list of "to-dos" that left me as I finally drifted off to sleep the previous night, the day ahead already feeling like a burden before I get out of bed.

As the day continues, different emotions can often creep in, whether we like it or not. And while it seems far easier to push them away (we've got so much to do, after all!), these feelings can tell us about what's happening deep within ourselves. The pilgrim who looks for the Sacred in the quotidian knows this, and as these everyday emotions enter in, she seeks to become aware of them, knowing they can tell her something more of herself, her daily journey, and often of her greater quest.

In today's meditation, you'll explore the emotions that have decided to greet you this morning and go deeper with them, meditating on what extraordinary things they might be telling you even in the ordinariness of your day-to-day.

Guided Meditation

Find a comfortable spot free of distraction and have your journal close by. Settle in with a few moments of silence and steady breathing and then direct your mind to the emotions that have decided to greet you today. Some might be obvious, such as worry that already has your mind racing or relief brought about by a slow morning ahead. Other emotions might be lurking in the background, not as easily translatable but still present, such as shame or sadness.

Take a few moments to explore these emotions, not going too deeply, just simply noticing their presence. As you notice them, acknowledge and welcome them, no matter how uncomfortable or unsettling they might be.

close your eyes and explore your emotions for a few minutes,
welcoming them

Now go a bit deeper with the emotions present, especially the ones that are surprising or strange, and begin to wonder what they might be trying to tell you. Do this internally first, making space for the Sacred Guide to give you insight rather than allowing your analytical brain to take over.

close your eyes again and spend a few minutes wondering

about what your emotions might be trying to say

Close your meditation with a breath of gratitude for your emotions and what they communicate to you, and then write down any new discoveries as a reminder of what your feelings can convey.

PRACTICE

As you go about your day, carry the purpose of this meditation with you in your heart. Become aware of your emotions as they arise, welcoming them and finding Sacred meaning within. You might be surprised at the wisdom found in things so seemingly ordinary.

REFLECTION

How can you begin to welcome your emotions as they come to you each day rather than rejecting them or pushing them away?

week one: day three

HOME

You might not use the word *ritual* everyday. In fact, images of strangers dancing around a fire in the light of the full moon might be playing through your mind. Perhaps you're more comfortable with the term *tradition*, but the truth is that ritual and tradition go hand in hand.

To better understand what a ritual really is, let's look at the definitions of ritual and tradition so we can know the difference between the two. A tradition is "something that is handed down ... from generation to generation."[3] A ritual is "a repetitive behavior" often practiced for the purpose of observance.[4] Tradition is about *remembering*, while ritual is about *enacting*.

What these two terms have in common is that they are both about making meaning. Tradition focuses on carrying on meaning from the past, while ritual is about creating meaning in the present. The pilgrim knows this and uses rituals to help him in his search for the Sacred within the quotidian. Through ritualization and enacting meaning, ordinary moments for the pilgrim can become moments of intention and Sacred Encounter.

PRACTICE

You can easily create meaning at home in your ordinary moments. Here are a few ways to ritualize the quotidian moments that are a part of life at home, inviting the Sacred into those ordinary places:

- *When you wake up and wash your face*, bringing refreshment for the new day, splash your face three times: in the name of the Creator, Christ, and the Sacred Guide.

- *Many people start their day with a hot cup* of coffee or tea. Instead of drinking it absentmindedly while watching the news, find a quiet place to sip from your cup, being present with each delicious drop. (It's manna from heaven after all, isn't it? It's the least you could do.)

- *Prepare dinner at night without any distractions,* finding relief in the steady rhythm of the chop-chop-chopping of the knife on the cutting board. It might very well be the first silence you've experienced all day. You can either savor the silence or use that time to pray or reflect over things you're grateful for in the day you've just experienced. Try this with other tasks that take some time but must be done, like washing the dishes or mowing the lawn.

- *If you go around locking doors and closing windows* before you go to bed each night, ritualize your physical actions toward safety as a prayer for your soul's protection for the following day against whatever might lead you away from your truest self and the Sacred.

REFLECTION

What is one regular aspect of your day that you can turn into a Sacred ritual?

week one: day four

WORK

As HUMAN BEINGS WITH a longing for the Sacred written on our hearts, we all desire purpose. For many, purpose is often sought through something that fills our everyday and colors our life journey: the workplace. But even the most passion-infused vocations can become mundane and tedious in the everyday, and whether you spend your days crunching numbers or leading future generations, it's easy to miss the presence of the Sacred within this ordinary aspect of our everyday lives.

In order to see the Sacred, then, you must have the proper eyes. Another way to describe this is your *lens*: the way in which you see the world. But to begin finding the Sacred in the quotidian, you must begin to practice. Just as you might have to wear glasses to help you see more clearly, in order to begin seeing the Sacred in seemingly ordinary places, you must put on lenses of Sacred-seeing. I like to call them *Pilgrim Glasses*.

The pilgrim on a journey away from home is well aware of her desire for God, so she's on the lookout for the Sacred around every corner. What she eats, where she rests her head, with whom she shares enriching conversation or even a simple greeting—these are ordinary things, and yet they are essential to the pilgrim.

The pilgrim knows that which is essential and life-giving is always of God, the source of life itself. She begins to see the Sacred not only in the provision for her daily needs as she journeys abroad, but also in the life-giving encounters at home and at work: a lunch break shared with a dear friend, a sincere greeting exchanged with colleagues as she walks through the door, or a thank you note from someone she recently served. These glimpses of the Sacred in ordinary moments remind her that meaning can be found in the everyday, too.

Because we each have different experiences, our perspective of where we find the Sacred in ordinary places can be unique, which is ultimately a gift to be shared. Sometimes we will be more aware than others of the presence of the Sacred or the potential for meaning found in our daily lives and work, and it is important to invite others into that Sacred presence. In the same way, I know there are many days when I'm distracted or stressed—not able to pay attention to the Sacred surrounding me—and the gentle prodding of a friend who has an eye for the Sacred amidst chaos helps call me back to what matters most.

PRACTICE

During your workday today, begin to notice the Sacred that surrounds you. You can keep a list at your desk or turn it into a fun exercise by trying on Pilgrim Glasses through the lens of a camera. Take a camera with you to work and begin capturing images of the Sacred ordinary. When you're on the lookout, viewing life through the lens of a pilgrim, you'll be surprised by what you discover, even if it is in a cubicle.

Don't know where to start? Take pictures of things that intrigue and surprise you. Even though you're now looking through Pilgrim Glasses, you're still seeing the world through your eyes, experience, and passions.

REFLECTION

How has this exercise showed you the Sacred in your work each day in ways you might not have seen otherwise?

week one: day five

COMMUNITY

FOR MOST OF US, community is a part of everyday life. It's formed through a group of friends or family, an organization in which we're involved, or by everyday environments, such as work or school. Community can even be found with your regular vendors at the farmers' market or at the age-old gathering places, known for their love of chatter and gossip: the salon or the barber shop.

No matter the communities in which we find ourselves on a daily basis, each offers an opportunity to experience the Divine. Since community is all about relationship, the meeting of two hearts and souls always presents us with an opportunity for Sacred Encounter.

In pilgrimage, this meeting of two hearts and souls is often described as *synchronicity*: an encounter by both necessity and chance. Synchronicity is also used to describe other serendipitous encounters: Right when you think you can walk no more, a bench appears around the corner. You're low on cash and need someplace to stay, only to find that you have just enough to pay for the last room in the village. You run into the station, thinking you've missed your train, but in fact it, too, has been delayed. The mere chance of these moments seems Sacred indeed, but perhaps the most powerful form of synchronicity happens in relationship with others, when two paths converge at just the moment where one can be most meaningful to the other.

Here's an example. I recently began to collaborate with a woman about our common work around the practice of pilgrimage. We initially connected in a way that seemed out of the blue, as is common with the Internet. However, after a while I had this strange sense that I somehow knew her. It turns out that we had in fact met once before—years ago at a yard sale. The most significant interaction I had with her then was when I paid for a few items.

While my passion for pilgrimage was gestating inside of me at the time, it had not yet been fully realized. I wasn't quite ready for our paths to fully intersect, as far as Divine plans were concerned. It was not yet time for the moment of synchronicity, when our hearts and our souls would meet with our common passion and desire. Fast forward three years later and our collaboration seems to be more significant than two people who stumbled upon each other. It feels destined in this moment in time—a Divine chance, a Sacred Encounter.

PRACTICE

You can start to look for the Sacred in your own community by paying attention to the relationships that you share, as well as those you witness around you. It can be found wherever there is a meeting of hearts and souls. It shows up in bouts of laughter and celebrations filled with joy. It can be seen in expressions of hope and pregnant moments bursting with desire. It is whispered in intimate conversations where struggles and heartache are shared. It is present especially in those long, silent moments, when we are comfortable enough with ourselves and with a relationship to be beside another person, simply in silence. And, Pilgrim, when hearts and souls meet in a moment of necessity and chance, you just might find yourself experiencing synchronicity.

REFLECTION

Are there any relationships or instances in your own journey that feel like synchronicity was or is at play?

week one: day six

NIGHT

THIS WEEK WE'VE BEEN focusing on finding the Sacred in the quotidian. Sometimes, though, the reality is that it's simpler to identify these things in retrospect. Whether our days seem long or short, routine or chaotic, it's easy to pass the day without noticing the Sacred, even with the best intentions. If this happens, no need to worry. Even though recognizing the Sacred in the present can help us to realize the beauty and wonder in the here and now, you'll find that when you look back after a weary day, the Sacred moments are still there.

In fact, while it is valuable for the pilgrim to recognize the Sacredness of the ordinary in the present moment, the practice of reflection is especially important for the pilgrim and her journey. While on the journey, the pilgrim might be so engrossed in the present moment that she cannot yet see the greater story and the transformation that the Sacred Guide is working from within. With trials and challenges around every corner, highs and lows, continuous surprises, and encounters that are beyond words (not to mention stretches when the journey simply seems quite dull), reflection helps the pilgrim begin to articulate her mystical experience upon return.

In a similar manner, sometimes we don't notice the fullness of

God's presence in our day-to-day lives until we reflect on it in retrospect. You can do this at the end of the day by asking a simple question: "Where have I seen God today?" A play on the Ignatian practice of *examen*, this practice will reveal to you the presence of the Sacred in your daily life in places you might never have noticed otherwise.

PRACTICE

As you settle down for the evening, or even as you're lying in bed drifting off to sleep, reflect on the experiences of your day—exciting and mundane—starting at the beginning and scanning for a sense of Sacred Encounter. Here are a few questions to help get your juices flowing:

- "Whom did I encounter today that reminded me of the Sacred?"
- "How did I experience God while at work?"
- "Have I seen glimpses of the Divine in my relationships with my family?"
- "Where did I see God in nature?"
- "Did I sense a Sacred connection with a stranger today?"

You can also uncover impressions of the Sacred by reflecting on what the best moments of your day were. I'm a firm believer that when we have life-giving experiences, we are also encountering God, the Giver of life. When you start to uncover themes within your moments of Sacred Encounter, consider intentionally seeking out similar moments. They are valuable and Sacred slices of your day.

REFLECTION

So, where did you see God today?

week one: day seven

GO FURTHER...

Intentionally seeking the Sacred in the quotidian can truly transform our everyday moments into times filled with meaning. And when we transform the way we see our days, we transform the way we spend our lives, however seemingly "ordinary." Here are some additional ways you can practice the first Pilgrim Principle, looking for the Sacred in the quotidian in the morning, at home, at work, in your community, and at night:

Morning: Practice gratitude
No need to reserve this for Thanksgiving. Practicing gratitude not only helps us to recognize the Sacred in the quotidian—it also allows us to express the positive impact that even the small and ordinary things can have on our well-being. In fact, practicing gratitude makes us more positive people. My theory? It's because practicing gratitude awakens us to life's Sacred gifts. Start practicing gratitude by keeping a gratitude journal or listing the five things you're grateful for each morning after you wake up. You might be surprised by how many things you are grateful for that are seemingly ordinary.

Home: Turn an ordinary space into a Sacred space

Whether we realize it or not, our environment has an impact on how we feel. This means that our surroundings can also invite us into a place of Sacred awareness. Think about it: it's a lot easier to be aware of the Sacred in a beautiful cathedral or a lush garden, right? And it's certainly a lot simpler to feel relaxed and intentional in a spa-like atmosphere that is soothing and calls you to be present. Perhaps you want to feel awake and joyful in your ordinary moments, and so you'd like to surround yourself with things that you love. Consider the ordinary places in which you do daily tasks, such as your kitchen or laundry room, and turn them into places that bring you life and delight.

Work: Take Sacred pauses throughout your day

Sometimes, to find the Sacred in the ordinary we have to take regular breaks. (In fact, it was during a much-needed break that I realized this!) Even though our days seem ordinary, they can still be chaotic. It's especially during the chaos that we need a reminder to step away, take a break, and recognize the Sacred still present all around us even though we've forgotten. Identify the most chaotic moments in your workday and choose to pause for at least 5-10 minutes after a hectic task is complete—slow down, quiet your mind, and just breathe. You can also set an alarm to go off each day during a moment when you know things become really hectic and you could use a reminder to invite you back to your awareness of the Sacred (4:30 in the afternoon, perhaps?).

Community: Share your ordinary moments with someone

Carpool with a colleague to work, sit down for a family meal, or exercise with friends instead of alone. If God is a relational being and we bear the Divine's image, then certainly we can experience the Sacred through one another.

Night: Live by candlelight after the sun sets

Candlelight always has a way of bringing us calm and turning us toward the Sacred. Consider spending an evening out of your week living by candlelight and reflect on how it makes you feel as you end the day. You could also try turning off the lights and lighting candles around the house just before bed, leading you into a Sacred slumber.

REFLECTION

What are some ways you've begun to practice the first Pilgrim Principle in your life this past week? How has this impacted your spirituality and daily journey?

week two

A PILGRIM PRACTICES SOMATIC SPIRITUALITY

week two: day one

INTRODUCTION

THIS WEEK WE'RE TAKING what we've learned from finding the Sacred in the ordinary and applying it to what just might be the most ordinary thing of all: *our bodies*. Historically, many have considered our bodies to be too ordinary to even matter to the spiritually enlightened. Our bodies are earthly, they say, and are plagued with sickness and disease. And isn't it the "flesh" that traps us within our sinful nature? If our bodies aren't going to be a part of the kingdom of God fulfilled, then certainly they have no spiritual value, right?

This is what the gnostics believed long ago, and while many aren't claiming the heretical title of "gnostic" anymore, this is the way the body is treated in many belief systems today. However, those belief systems just don't jive with the pilgrim, who knows that the body is a key player in the journey.

It is the body that carries the pilgrim from one place to another and the senses that serve as a conduit for the many cultural and spiritual experiences that permeate her being along the way. Even in the interior journey, the pilgrim knows that external sensations can help guide her to her core. In fact, if there weren't any bodily significance in physical pilgrimage, then it wouldn't serve as such a powerful metaphor for our journeys in life, would it?

This is where somatic spirituality comes in. In order understand what somatic spirituality looks like, it's good to first know what somatic means:

so•mat•ic [soh-**mat**-ik], *adjective*[5]
1. of the body; bodily; physical

And so, *somatic spirituality* is simply a faith that incorporates the body as a vital participant and resource in our spiritual search.

Need an example? If you grew up in a Christian family, it is likely that you have been trained spiritually in words, whether by reading the Bible, Scripture memorization, conversation, or prayer. While each of these things is valuable, some days you might find yourself feeling exhausted by all of the words, longing to practice a faith where you can connect spiritually—and sometimes far more profoundly—in other ways. God did not create us with only a mind and call us "good"—God also created us with bodies that can be vessels of spiritual expression as well as reception.

Our bodies carry just as much wisdom and insight as our minds. In fact, our bodies have the ability to tell us truths about our condition that our minds won't allow to surface as we try to maintain control. The pilgrim on a physical journey knows this truth, engaging holistically in the practice of pilgrimage by incorporating not only the mind, but also the body in her spiritual search.

Even though you cannot realistically travel to far off lands each day, you can still holistically journey daily as a pilgrim by practicing somatic spirituality. In this week's readings, we'll explore ways you can enhance your spiritual practice through each of the five senses: hearing, touch, smell, sight, and taste.

REFLECTION

In what ways do you already use your body in your spiritual practice? If somatic spirituality is new to you, what feelings do you have about incorporating your body into your search for the Divine?

week two: day two

HEARING

In TODAY'S MEDITATION, you're going to experience a refreshing way to engage the Scripture through *lectio divina*. *Lectio divina* is an ancient spiritual practice meaning "sacred reading" and is often practiced in silence. However, it can also become an audible experience by reading the passage out loud. Engaging your sense of hearing through listening to Scripture—something commonly read silently—can help you experience the passage in a new way.

Although *lectio divina* is rooted in the Christian tradition, it doesn't have to be used exclusively when reading the Bible. You can also use it with a favorite poem, song, or passage from another spiritual book. No matter what medium you use when practicing *lectio divina*, what remains the same is this: it is a practice that is guided by the Divine.

In today's meditation, you'll practice *lectio divina* using a passage from 1 Kings chapter 19. It is the story of Elijah's strange encounter with God in the wilderness, and I've chosen it because of the way Elijah ultimately experienced God's passing by: as a gentle whisper, something that required careful listening in more ways than one.

Guided Meditation

To begin, make sure you're in a comfortable, quiet place and have all the resources you need, including a journal in which to write down any insight at the end of your time that came to you during your practice.

STEP 1: LECTIO (READ)

Go through the passage a few times, either reading it out loud slowly or listening to a recording with your eyes closed, pausing between each reading to allow the passage to sink in. As you read or listen, pay attention to any phrases that stand out to you and hold onto them loosely. You'll need them for step two: *meditatio* (meditate).

1 Kings 19:9b-13

9bThe word of the Lord came to him: "What are you doing here, Elijah?"

10He replied, "I have been very zealous for the Lord God Almighty. The Israelites have rejected your covenant, torn down your altars, and put your prophets to death with the sword. I am the only one left, and now they are trying to kill me too."

11The Lord said, "Go out and stand on the mountain in the presence of the Lord, for the Lord is about to pass by."

Then a great and powerful wind tore the mountains apart and shattered the rocks before the Lord, but the Lord was not in the wind. After the wind there was an earthquake, but the Lord was not in the earthquake. 12After the earthquake came a fire, but the Lord was not in the fire. And after the fire came a gentle whisper. 13When Elijah heard it, he pulled his cloak over his face and went out and stood at the mouth of the cave.

Then a voice said to him, "What are you doing here, Elijah?"

read/listen to the passage at least three times,
pausing between each reading

STEP 2: MEDITATIO (MEDITATE)

Now it's time to focus in on the phrase that stood out to you. Bring the phrase to mind and meditate on it. Repeat the phrase in your mind slowly, noticing what emerges for you. As thoughts and feelings surface, let them sink in without distracting you from your meditation—the phrase might still have more to give.

close your eyes and spend a few minutes
meditating on what stood out to you

STEP 3: ORATIO (PRAY)

As you transition from meditation to prayer, begin communicating with God about the phrase from your meditation. Explore what made the phrase stand out initially and share any feelings that came up for you during your meditation. As you share these things in prayer, take note of any new insight you are given in regards to the text as well as what has been awakened in you through your phrase.

close your eyes and spend a few minutes in prayer,
exploring your experience

STEP 4: CONTEMPLATIO (CONTEMPLATE)

As your prayer comes to a close, spend some time in God's presence contemplating what has happened within you throughout this time of reading, meditation, and prayer. Bring to mind any new insights you've received during this time, whether personal or in relation to the text, and let them sink in, coloring your way of being. Write these things down in your journal, as well as any reflections you have on using your sense of hearing to experience something you would often have only read silently. In the end, you might be surprised how listening to a passage or reading it out loud can offer you a different perspective than if you had only read it to yourself.

spend some time reflecting on your experience

After your period of contemplation, bring your practice to a close with some deep breathing, a prayer, or simply a few more moments in silence.

PRACTICE

Consider making *lectio divina* a regular practice, exploring what it's like both with Scripture and beyond, such as your favorite poem or song. It might give you intriguing insight into why the poem or song continues to resonate with you so deeply.

REFLECTION

What new insight did you receive through today's *lectio divina*? If this is a new practice for you, how did it offer you a new way to experience the Divine?

week two: day three

TOUCH

YESTERDAY WE PRACTICED somatic spirituality by engaging in Scripture in a new way: listening. There are many other ways we can engage our bodies in the practices we are already familiar with. In fact, engaging things in alternative ways often gives us new perspectives. That's why we have the phrase "shake things up," right?

Today, let's do just that and shake things up with one of the most common spiritual practices: prayer. I grew up in a tradition where I was encouraged to pray from an early age, particularly at mealtimes and bedtime: *"God is great, God is good, let us thank him for our food...,"* and *"Now I lay me down to sleep, I pray the Lord my soul to keep...."* Perhaps you know these prayers, too.

Or maybe you grew up in a more liturgical tradition, memorizing and reciting prayers of old: *"Our Father in heaven, hallowed be thy name...,"* or *"Hail Mary, full of grace, the Lord is with thee...."* There are many beautiful psalms and prayers written by biblical figures and saints alike, giving us guidance and words when we need them most.

As I grew older, my prayer life expanded in my evangelical world to include praises and requests (not to mention the ever-elusive "unspoken"). We kept prayer journals and were encouraged to be prayer warriors. My prayers no longer included childlike rhymes but rather began with *"Dear God"* (I was never a *"Heavenly Father"* person, but it was an equally accepted and appropriate beginning), and always *always* ended with *"In Jesus' name I pray."* Anything in the middle was spur-of-the-moment and fair game and was given bonus points for flowery language.

This type of prayer can be beautiful and moving, no doubt (though the flowery stuff is more fluff). But I was mistaken to think that this was the only way to pray. In fact, I found that my prayers so easily fit into a mold that I began to become exhausted by them. I needed a fresh and new way to connect with God—one that required intention, yes, but also didn't leave me breathless and drained. And most important, I needed a prayer practice that allowed me more space to simply offer my full self in the presence of the Divine rather than just speaking.

As I expressed in this week's introduction, at times we are without words to pray, and yet we still long to connect with the Sacred. One way that you can do this is by incorporating touch and movement into your spiritual practice. When you do this, you are establishing contact with the Sacred in a physical way, whether by dancing to the music within your soul or burrowing your feet deep into the sand. Through these physical acts, we are presenting both a plea for connection and an offering of ourselves toward Sacred Encounter. Isn't that what prayer is about, anyway?

PRACTICE

Try offering your presence in a different way by going on a prayer walk (or run!). As you leave, pray that the rhythm of your steps will offer the prayers that your soul cannot speak, and then walk—for 20 minutes or even an hour—in the presence of the Divine, simply as an offering.

REFLECTION

What was it like to pray using touch and movement rather than words today? Was it a struggle? Did you feel a sense of relief?

week two: day four

SMELL

IF THERE WERE EVER A sense that you think wouldn't be spiritually inspiring, this might be it. But the sense of smell is more influential than you might think. In fact, scent is commonly linked with memory.

There are a few scents that are especially strong for me, bringing forth memories in an instant—or rather, transporting me back to those places long ago. The smell of cut grass will always remind me of summer and hamburgers cooking on a grill. When I have a pot of vegetable soup simmering on the stove, I can close my eyes and be taken to my childhood, arriving home from school on a crisp fall day, backpack in tow. I also find comfort and delight in the particular scent of places—homes of friends and family, underground transportation, school hallways—locations where I can close my eyes, breathe in, and know exactly where I am. (Step into the natural foods section at a grocery store and you'll know exactly what I mean.)

Strong scents can capture us in such a powerful way that they have the power to transport us, which is why the sense of smell can be a valuable tool for the pilgrim in search of the Sacred. In fact, scent has been used for thousands of years in religious rituals, particularly in the form of incense.

Most often used today in high liturgical traditions during the distribution of the Eucharist, the incorporation of incense within ritual is more than simply an embellishment. When used during the ritual, something both physically and spiritually significant occurs: the scent of incense transports you to a Sacred place and offers a somatic experience which mirrors the internal connection with the Divine during Sacred Encounter. As you breathe in the unique and strong fragrance of the incense, you symbolically take in the presence of the Divine. In turn, you are present through the stimulation of the senses. As the incense burns, the smoke rises upward toward what has traditionally been viewed as the heavens, serving as an offering and invitation for Divine participation. Alongside the Divine, you are stimulated, present, active. And in this communal space, you are united with the Sacred.

Having grown up in the evangelical tradition, I didn't experience this until attending an Anglo-Catholic church in Seattle. However, it quickly grew to be one of my favorite elements of the service. Music and readings have always been a part of services I participated in, but the stimulation of my sense of smell was entirely new. Now, just as with certain scents connected with my past, each time I encounter incense in a spiritual setting, breathing it in, I am transported to a Sacred place.

PRACTICE

You can use your sense of smell to remember and be transported to a place of Sacred intention, too. Try lighting a scented candle or burning a certain fragrance of incense while you do your spiritual practices each day.

You could also carry something with you, such as a sachet, to return you to your center and remind you of the presence of the Sacred, even during your daily tasks. Aromatherapy can help you to choose a scent based on how you want to feel. For example, lavender and vanilla are said to calm and relieve stress, rosemary and peppermint are often connected to memory and sharpening the mind, and citrus scents can bring energy and brighten moods.

REFLECTION

What unique scents capture your attention, drawing you closer toward the Sacred?

week two: day five

SIGHT

OF ALL OF THE SENSES, it is probably the most common to experience the Divine through sight. The created world is filled with unending inspiration, and there is no doubt that sweeping views of rugged mountain ranges or endless seas were imagined by a Being who begets awe. Even the sight of things made by human hands can illicit Sacred Encounter—a cavernous cathedral, perhaps, its stained glass casting colored rays that fall upon an altar. Images of far off places help to inspire journeys; paintings viewed in a gallery remind us that the life's Sacred questions existed long before our time.

But the pilgrim who is at home doesn't necessarily spend his days walking through galleries or sitting in cathedrals. Our daily life, as we've already explored, can be rather mundane without the intention of finding the Sacred. We wake up, work, run errands, raise families, and at the end of the day numb ourselves to the ordinariness of it all, having lost sight of the Divine's presence in life.

While we have lost sight on a grander scale—the awareness of and search for the Sacred forgotten or thwarted—we can literally use our *sight* as a way of introducing ourselves to the Divine presence both around and within us once again. During our exploration of the

Sacred in our everyday lives last week, we did this by viewing our workdays through the lens of pilgrimage, or *Pilgrim Glasses*. Another way our sight can guide us to the Sacred is through the use of icons.

Since the early days of Christianity, artists have been creating icons to call us back into the presence of the Divine. In fact, icons are referred to as windows or doors unto heaven, the soul, *the Sacred*. The significance of icons is not only in the images we see hanging on a cathedral wall or perched on a bookshelf at home. The spiritual influence begins long before the last brush stroke. So much intention goes into the creation of icons that there is even a specific title for those who lend their talents to the art. These artists are called *iconographers*, and they are true seers, studying the particular language of iconography and finding ancient stories and images filled with meaning to portray. As they create, they treat their brushstrokes as a prayer for those who will one day gaze upon the icon, hungry for the Sacred.

Once the icon is finished, its spiritual significance is carried on by those who look upon the icon in prayer and meditation. Just as the iconographer is the seer who prepares the doorway, *you* are the seer who gazes with intention, ready to enter. Focusing on an icon uniquely allows your sight to guide you into prayer and meditation, centering yourself as you encounter the Divine.

PRACTICE

Add an icon to an area in your home where you're in need of a doorway to the Divine. Or, use your sight to discover other created things that serve as a window to the Divine, such as a mighty tree or a flowing stream. Just as you would with an icon, don't simply glance at it and pass by, but rather stay with it, allowing it to transport you to the Sacred.

REFLECTION

What images can you add to your altar or Sacred space that can act as an icon—a window to the Divine?

week two: day six

TASTE

FOOD IS COMMONLY understood as a necessity in life for our physical nourishment, but it has long been a source of spiritual nourishment as well. I'm not talking about that tub of ice cream you pull out of the freezer at the end of a bad day or the bag of chips you completely devour while sitting on the couch. Whether we want to admit it or not, I think we all know that any nourishment we get from such over-indulgences is fleeting. While the first bite might taste heavenly, our thoughts inevitably take over and we eat absentmindedly. In such instances we are not present, we are not aware, and we are warding off spiritual nourishment rather than receiving it.

When I talk about the spiritual nourishment that comes from food, I'm envisioning long dinners at the table surrounded by friends. I'm thinking of the rich simmering soup you make for your family on a cold winter's night. And I'm imagining the taste of a blackberry picked fresh from a wild bush in the summertime, bursting with flavor. Each of these instances can nourish the spirit, and each involves taste in some way or another.

The pilgrim is quite familiar with taste—in the metaphorical way, at least. To even have set off on a journey, the pilgrim must have tasted something of the Divine, leaving him longing for more. Often such a taste can be fleeting, but it awakens the senses and sparks desire. For the pilgrim committed to his journey, this is only a foretaste, for it is a glimpse of the goodness yet to come along the road.

To savor these tastes, the pilgrim must exercise the senses, and in a way, that's what we've been doing all week. By connecting to the Sacred through hearing, touch, smell, and sight, we have been sharpening our senses and manifesting externally what we long to experience internally. This can be done through tasting, too. When we taste something—*savor* it, slowly and truly—we inhale its goodness and by it are blessed. Surely, as we learn to savor the simple blessing of food, we will learn to fully savor life's Sacred Encounters as well.

PRACTICE

Perhaps the greatest thing about practicing somatic spirituality—using our bodies and our senses with the intention of Sacred Encounter—is that when we are engaging the senses, we can be fully present. Today, find a food or drink you love and taste it—*fully, slowly, silently savor it*—being present to your every delight, and know that where you delight and savor, you will truly taste the Divine.

REFLECTION

What was it like to be present while eating, savoring both the moment and the flavor of your food or drink?

week two: day seven

GO FURTHER...

SINCE WE ALL ENGAGE our bodies in different ways, the possibilities for using them in our spiritual practices are endless. My hope is that you find a way to practice somatic spirituality that feels true to you, but I also hope that you aren't afraid to try something new as well.

As you explore and invent new ways to incorporate your body into your spiritual practice, be creative! Anything that has to do with hearing, touch, smell, sight, and taste is fair game (within moral reason, of course!). To give you ideas, here are some more ways to practice somatic spirituality right at home through the senses of hearing, touch, smell, sight, and taste:

Hearing: Listen to instrumental music

Listening to instrumental music can take you out of your head and into the present moment where you are better aware of your true self and can more fully experience the Divine. Try listening to instrumental music as a morning practice or when sitting in stillness at the end of your day. You can go classical or try something more modern, such as Helios or Nils Frahm (two of my current favorites).

Touch: Pray while holding a tactile object

You can do this the traditional way, with a rosary or prayer beads (you can easily find instructions for praying with these objects online), or you could hold something that represents your intention. Not surprisingly, we often find ourselves praying in times of chaos, so rubbing a smooth stone or holding on to a comforting pillow can help ease you into prayer and be a physical reminder of the Divine's peaceful presence.

Smell: Attend a service where incense is used

To experience first hand how the sense of smell has been incorporated in ritual for thousands of years, attend a service where incense is used. You're most likely to find it in high liturgical churches, especially on significant days within the liturgical calendar, such as Christmas Day or Easter Sunday.

Sight: Visit a church filled with stained glass windows

Stained glass has adorned churches for centuries. One of the interesting things about the art of stained glass is that you can't appreciate it to its fullest unless you are inside the church. When you view the composition from the inside, light shines through the colored glass, illuminating the scene. I especially love it when rays of color from the stained glass can be found shimmering throughout the sanctuary. Even in its simplicity, it seems so Sacred.

Taste: Eat a food straight off the vine

(Or the tree, or the bush—you get my drift.) Food is an essential part of everyday, and it's so important to remember that though it seems so ordinary, it comes from a Sacred source. Encounter that Sacred source through the sense of taste by picking and eating something ripe and fresh. The flavor is absolutely unmatched.

REFLECTION

What are some ways you've begun to practice the second Pilgrim Principle in your life this past week? How has this impacted your spirituality and daily journey?

week three

A PILGRIM IS A GOOD
STEWARD OF RESOURCES

week three: day one

INTRODUCTION

To some, being a good steward of resources has nothing to do with spirituality. In fact, many people don't think about being good stewards of their resources at all. You might say that they are unaware of the value of the resources at their disposal. But awareness is a key practice for the pilgrim, and in fact is a necessary part of each Pilgrim Principle. The pilgrim who is aware of the true value of her resources knows that they are gifts from the Divine—tools that may seem inconsequential, but can help her along the journey.

Consider the ancient pilgrims in the Middle Ages, who would be gone for months or years at a time with the revered purpose of journeying to a Sacred site. While their goals were spiritual in nature—well beyond the practical realm—their basic needs still had to be met. They carried little with them—a coat, a small satchel for money, and maybe a walking stick—and they depended on the provision of others for many resources along the way.

Pilgrims were often given food and shelter in monasteries on the path. They took meals where they could find them and continued on their journey each day, not knowing where they would lay their heads next. But they knew that somehow the necessary resources would be provided and that their basic needs would be met in one way or another. Having set everything aside to make the journey, these pilgrims were simply grateful for any resource given, considering it provision from God.

Today, many of us have more resources than we could ever need. Indeed, it's a blessing to have abundance, but to truly be aware of this abundance, we must also practice good stewardship, and this starts at home. To the pilgrim, being a good steward of resources is not just about money, but also time, abilities, possessions, and the environment. Being a good steward of resources is vital for the pilgrim, not only because she has committed to a life of simplicity and responsibility on the road, but also particularly at home, for it is being a good steward in daily life that allows the pilgrim to go on journeys.

What does it mean to be a good steward of resources? It means practicing presence and recognizing you have time in abundance. It means offering your unique gifts to the world and using them as tools in your journey. It means not spending more money than you have and giving freely of what you do have. It means regularly purging yourself of unnecessary possessions and only holding on to things that are useful, whether in a utilitarian manner or simply because they bring you joy and delight. And, of course, it means awareness of our responsibility for the earth, which has been left in our care.

This week we're going to begin practicing awareness of our abundant resources, including time, money, abilities, possessions, and the environment, exploring ways that we can be good stewards right at home. They might seem basic at first, but becoming a good steward of resources will help you to journey more simply as a pilgrim and teach you to be aware of the value of these resources along the road.

REFLECTION

What are some areas in which you could better steward your resources?

week three: day two

TIME

TIME IS SOMETHING THAT we all have, but can never have enough of. *We're running out of time, we didn't have time, we can't find the time.* In other situations, it seems there's too much time—*it took a while, we had to wait for a long time,* and on and on. We also *spend* or *save* time, as if it's a commodity, and even *kill* time, as if it's under our control.

But what is a journey without the passing of time? For the pilgrim, time is especially important for the process of transformation. It is a key ingredient in the practice of pilgrimage, and yet this ingredient is not in the human terms mentioned above. Rather, time is experienced through the lens of the Sacred, who transcends time. To the Sacred, time is abundant and serves as rich soil for transformation. To fully embrace the transformation that each journey brings just as the pilgrim does, we must then learn to value time as an abundant resource. But to truly cherish this abundance, we must first become aware of our relationship with time.

Guided Meditation

In today's meditation, we're going to explore our relationship with time, Charles Dickens-style. Inviting the presence of the Holy Spirit—our *Sacred Guide*—we'll visit the past, present, and future, looking at how we spend time, when we wish we had more time, and naming how we can use time as a resource along the journey.

Find a comfortable place free of distractions. Start by simply settling the mind for a few moments in silence (since, as I said before, we have time in abundance). Close your eyes and slowly breathe in and out, sinking into the present moment, and invite the Sacred Guide to join you on this journey. After some moments of centering, we'll begin our journey into the past.

pause, centering for a minute or so

Continue to breathe in and out deeply as we journey into the past. Reflect on your relationship with time so far. Does it feel like an abundant resource, or have you often felt like you were running out of time?

Notice the feelings that come up as you reflect over your relationship with time in the past. The feelings that arise as you look back probably indicate your relationship with time. Do you feel anxious? Restful and at peace? Sad or numb? How has time played a role in your journey? Stay for a few more minutes in the past with the Sacred Guide listening, feeling, and observing before we skip ahead into the future.

pause, reflecting on the past

Now, remembering your past relationship with time, journey with the Sacred Guide into the future. Imagine that you have time in abundance. Do you envision more spaciousness? What things fall away because you are no longer worried about time? Do you feel a sense of relief? What do you see yourself doing that you felt you didn't have time for in the past? Stay here for a few minutes more, savoring what it's like to experience time as an abundant resource.

pause, imagining the future

Now return to the present, having been reminded of your past relationship with time and envisioned what it could be like in the future. Think about your day and week ahead and what it will look like in relationship to time. What are some changes you could make to feel like your time is more abundant? If you feel pressed for time, what can you do to change your outlook? For a few minutes, think about how you can be more intentional with the resource of time today, cherishing the time you have and savoring the abundance in the present moment.

pause, picturing the present

As you draw your meditation to a close, re-enter your day with this new perspective of time as an abundant resource, allowing space for the Divine's mysterious movement and grace for your journey.

PRACTICE

The best way to truly value the time we have and to realize our abundance of time is to practice being present. When you find yourself wandering today, wishing you had more time or impatient that things are taking up too much time, let the Sacred Guide usher you back to the present—the only place time truly exists, and where it exists in abundance.

REFLECTION

In what ways can you better recognize the abundance of time? The places where you feel as though you don't have enough time are a good place to start.

week three: day three

MONEY

OF COURSE, IF WE'RE going to talk about resources, we have to talk about money. Money is a necessity in life and a resource used in exchange for many of the other resources we're exploring this week. We are given money for our time, and we pay money to save time. We are given money for our abilities and pay money to strengthen our abilities. We pay money for our possessions. And while there's not as direct a link between money and the environment, I have a feeling we'll be paying in the future for the ways we neglect the environment today, whether that's in money, time, possessions, or with our very lives.

Yes, money is a necessary resource, and it is required for the pilgrim as well. In fact, as I mentioned in this week's introduction, a satchel with coins was one of the only things the traditional pilgrim carried. Going out on a journey was a great expense for the pilgrim, and it still can be today. This is why it's important to remember that the ability to go on pilgrimage is a gift, and we must be conscious about how we spend our money, because, tragically, it is not a resource that everyone has.

When we are aware of how we spend our money, taking care to

spend it wisely and only within our means, we are more likely to see the opportunities it affords us as a gift. And when you begin to see the opportunity to go on pilgrimage as a gift and calling, you'll find the presence of the Sacred everywhere you turn.

Likewise, when we are conscious of how much money we spend, we can commit to giving money to others in order to support their own journeys in ways they might not have been able to otherwise. A donation to feed a child for a month or to help obtain clean drinking water for a village can bring wellness and long life to many whose journeys are hanging by a thread. Giving to a scholarship fund can change the lives of students preparing for careers in which they can truly make a difference. By financially contributing to those in need, you can become the hand of the Divine in another's life. You'll soon find that your donation will not only impact others' lives for the better—it will shape your own journey, too.

One more thing: since we're talking about money, I want to recognize the reality that many people feel that they don't have enough money to go on pilgrimage. However, I'm confident of this: if you long to go on pilgrimage and are committed to living on a budget, setting aside money each month to fund your journey, you can make it happen. That journey might be one or five years in the future, and it might amount to an around-the-world ticket or simply a journey to a nearby monastery, but it will happen if you're committed to it.

An added bonus? By purposefully setting aside money over time for your journey, giving up what isn't necessary in lieu of your search for the Sacred, you'll be cultivating the intention required along the road as well. With that in mind, the wait doesn't seem so bad after all, does it?

PRACTICE

Make the decision to invest in a journey, whether someone else's or your own. And remember, it doesn't necessarily have to be a physical journey. Many journeys don't involve leaving home. How can you creatively use the money you have to further a journey that you, a friend, or someone in need is on already?

REFLECTION

What is your relationship with money? How are you using this resource to support your own journeys or the journeys of others?

week three: day four

ABILITIES

WHEN TALKING ABOUT resources, we are more likely to think of time, money, possessions, and the environment than our abilities. In order to be good stewards, we must be attentive to these things, yes. But we often forget that our abilities deserve our attention and care as well. Perhaps this neglect comes from not truly knowing and celebrating our unique and given abilities. And when we aren't aware of our abilities, it is impossible to lean into them.

By abilities, I don't mean "proficiency in Microsoft Office" or "the ability to work with a team" that might end up under the "skills" section of your resumé. I'd like to leave those under the "skills" section here, too. What I'm talking about are God-given talents that correlate with our passions and call us toward something more—the things that have come so naturally that we can't explain it, leaving us filled with excitement and anticipation.

We each have been given many abilities as resources for the journey. Our abilities aren't our vocation, but when we lean into them, they can lead to it, creating a career path that we are uniquely suited for and that we might not have found if we had followed traditional means.

So what does it mean to "lean into our abilities," and how does this make us a good steward of this resource? To lean into our abilities is to *name them*, to *cultivate them*, and finally to *offer them* and step back to see what happens.

To name our abilities, we must discover not what skills have been developed, but rather, as mentioned before, those abilities which come most naturally to us—the ones whose source is unexplainable, and yet they make us come alive. Once we've named these abilities, we must cultivate them through engaging them—using them where relevant in any opportunity that arises. The last step as we lean into our abilities is to offer them and step back to see what happens. When we lean into our abilities and offer them back to the world, magic transpires and things take flight. If we are alert, new paths will be created, new creations born.

The pilgrim on a journey must be able to lean into his abilities, too, so that he is able to use them if and when the time comes. Even the creation of the journey itself is a result of the pilgrim's abilities. When the pilgrim starts to name what comes naturally to him and makes him come alive, he can also begin to know more of the journey that lies ahead of him. Once the journey begins, the pilgrim's abilities become tools in the journey, specialties that aid in times of trial, helping him to slay his personal dragons and continue on the path toward Sacred Encounter.

PRACTICE

Consider what it means for you to lean into your abilities—to name them, to cultivate them, and to offer them. If you're not sure what your unique abilities are, begin by asking a few people close to you what they think. Perhaps they see you as a good listener or as someone who inspires them to take action. Maybe you're the one they turn to when they need some extra hands or when they are looking for spiritual guidance.

If you already know of some of your abilities, commit to cultivating them, whether that means signing up for a class or finally sitting down to write. And, of course, once you've named your abilities and have begun to cultivate them, think creatively about how you might offer them. Then, step back and see what happens when you begin to offer what you can uniquely give to the world.

REFLECTION

What abilities do you have that you consider to be valuable resources? How can you begin to use them with intention to impact your journey and your community?

week three: day five

POSSESSIONS

In this week's introduction, I described the outfitting of the traditional pilgrim—coat, staff, and small satchel. Though times have changed and many advancements have been made in the travel gear market, one thing remains the same between the possessions of the traditional and modern pilgrim on a physical journey: they possess what they can carry.

This doesn't mean that they carry only the obvious necessities, though. Pilgrims today carry a change of clothes, soap, and a toothbrush, yes—but they also carry journals for reflection, books for inspiration, and photographs for remembrance. They might carry music for motivation or lip gloss to help them forget that they haven't showered in five days. These things can be just as important to the well-being of the pilgrim as a jacket to shield her from the rain or a broken-in pair of boots.

Of course, filling a single bag with both practical and personal necessities can quickly result in overpacking. I've heard many stories of pilgrims on the road to Santiago de Compostela deciding to leave things behind along the way that weren't so important after all, just to lighten the load. As they journeyed, learning more about themselves as well as the path on which they walked, they came to realize that they could do without the things that once seemed necessary. In fact, they felt better for it.

Being intentional with our possessions and lightening the load is something we can also practice in our daily lives as pilgrims. Though with the amount of possessions in our homes, it will take more than a split-second to decide what we can leave behind or let go. Whether you notice it or not, the possessions that surround you have a significant effect on your well-being, just as the weight of the pilgrim's possessions can impact her journey. All of our possessions have joined us on our journey at one point or another. Whether their arrival was met with excitement, obligation, or indifference, anything that continues to be in our possession is still with us on our journey, no matter how deep and dark the closet in which we try to hide it.

We could all benefit from lightening our load, as far as possessions are concerned. And as is the case with the pilgrim, that doesn't mean only keeping the things that are "necessary" in practical terms. It also means that we should hold onto the possessions that bring us life and nourish our souls, as mentioned in this week's introduction. Beauty and remembrance meet needs of their own. However, deciding what stays and what goes isn't an easy task. That's why (again, as with the pilgrim) we have to pay attention to our daily journeys in order to discern which possessions are of true value to us and which ones are ultimately a burden.

For many of us, lightening the load is a great task that can take hours, days, months, and maybe (gulp!) years. But it is a necessary task if we want to live as pilgrims in the everyday, being good stewards of our resources and conscious of our possessions. There are a lot of great suggestions out there about how to begin the minimizing process (there's even an entire minimalist movement), but it's up to you as to how to begin.

PRACTICE

Begin lightening your load right now by starting with just one thing a day. Each day, identify one thing that you don't need or use anymore and put it in an "outbox"—a designated box of things to sell, donate, or give to someone else. At the end of the month, get rid of the items inside. I have a feeling that if you start small like this, you'll find it to be an easy and liberating process, and you might just be surprised by the things you no longer need or desire as your journey continues.

REFLECTION

What are some possessions you have that enrich your journey, bringing you life? Which possessions are burdensome items whose absence would lighten your spiritual and emotional load? Take action by placing these things in your outbox today.

week three: day six

ENVIRONMENT

IT COULD BE SAID that the environment is the most significant resource we have in our possession, its value to us so great that it cannot be measured. In fact, it's not simply a single resource, but contains within it millions of resources that feed us, nourish us, move us, delight us, heal us—the list goes on and on.

Over the past many years, the need and responsibility to care for the environment has become more prevalent in Western culture. Environmentally-friendly methods are more common; recycling is a household practice in many homes; and *green* is now more than simply a color—*going green* (being environmentally conscious) is a quickly growing trend.

And yet somehow, many who say they believe in a Divine Creator—who in fact claim to be doing the work of God on Earth—have missed the message. The very people who are meant to be aware of God's presence and provision in everyday life seem to be ignoring their role in caring for the greatest resource given to them and one of the finest expressions of the Divine: the environment.

As a tribe always searching for the Sacred, we as pilgrims cannot afford to miss the presence and provision of the very thing we seek right in front of us. Practicing pilgrimage everyday and being a good steward of resources requires awareness of the responsibility we have to care for these resources and the many opportunities to do so that are within our grasp.

There are many ways to care for the environment right in your home. The well-known saying "reduce, reuse, recycle" is a great place to start. *Reduce* by using less—energy, water, plastic, disposable items. *Reuse* by repurposing where possible—plastic shopping bags as trash bags, glass jars as storage containers, old clothes and linens as rags. Finally, if you can't reduce the need of it or reuse it, *recycle* it: plastic, paper, cardboard, aluminum, glass—the list goes on. If you practice caring for the environment through reducing, reusing, and recycling, you'll find yourself throwing out very little waste in the end.

Of course, you might be wondering: "What does this have to do with the pilgrim?" That's a good question with an easy answer. Aside from the obvious reality that caring for the environment ultimately benefits the pilgrim and her community (as well as the places she is traveling), caring for the environment also makes us more aware of the presence of the Sacred echoing throughout all of creation. Additionally, by helping to sustain one of our greatest resources, environmental awareness continues to help cultivate intentionality. As with many other practices, caring for the environment and being a good steward of resources in everyday life will teach the pilgrim to be intentional on a daily basis, and only with intentionality can we set off on meaningful journeys.

PRACTICE

Start caring for the environment today by finding out what can be recycled in your community and setting a recycling bin right next to your trash can so you're prompted to think before you toss. Consider how you might be able to reuse things that can't be recycled easily, such as using the plastic bags you get at the store as trash bags (as suggested previously). Of course, you can reduce the use of plastic bags altogether by bringing your own reusable bags with you when you go shopping.

REFLECTION

What are a few small steps you can take to be a good steward of the environment each day?

week three: day seven

GO FURTHER...

THROUGHOUT THIS WEEK we've explored why it's important for the pilgrim to be a good steward of resources, as well as many ways we can better care for the resources that we have, including time, money, our abilities, our possessions, and the environment. Here are some suggestions to ensure that others benefit from the same resources as well:

Time: Give someone the day off

If you are an employer, a parent, or even a friend, you can give the gift of unexpected time in another person's life by giving someone time off, whether it's from a job, a responsibility, or an evening without children by offering to babysit.

Money: Give to someone in need

This is probably the most common way to offer resources, and it will always be needed. To be more involved in your giving, consider giving to an organization like kiva.org, where you can loan money to small business owners in developing countries. You can read stories, choose which business you want to fund, and track their progress.

When you are paid back for your investment, you can invest it again in another project and person you believe in.

Abilities: Offer your talents for free

Many of us have skills that we are paid to use (and even if we don't get paid for some, they're still of great value). Share your abilities with others by offering your skills and services for free to communities or organizations that you belong to. You can also pass on your abilities by teaching your well-refined skills to others.

Possessions: Send a care package

Sometimes, a little something tangible can mean the world. Whether it is a necessity or a keepsake, sending objects to those in need is a wonderful way to communicate love and support. Consider showing your support and love by sending care packages to soldiers, missionaries, aid workers, college students, and sick friends. There are also many ministries and organizations where you can help put together packages filled with things like school supplies and Christmas gifts for those in need around the world.

Environment: Pick up trash in your neighborhood

Sadly, not everyone is a great steward of the environment, and litter is prevalent in small towns and cities alike. Make a practice of picking up trash you see as you pass by and disposing of it properly. People might notice your intention and be reminded of the importance of caring for the environment. It's also a great opportunity to spend time outside!

REFLECTION

What are some ways you've begun to practice the third Pilgrim Principle in your life this past week? How has this impacted your spirituality and daily journey?

week four

A PILGRIM IMMERSES
HERSELF IN CULTURE

week four: day one

INTRODUCTION

TODAY YOU'VE REACHED the middle week of *Pilgrim Principles*. Can you believe you're almost halfway through? Fittingly, this week we're spending time with a principle that is best exercised in the middle stage of the pilgrimage, when the pilgrim has reached his destination, immersed in another culture and on the lookout for the Sacred.

There is a reason why the pilgrim's journey involves going somewhere else. In order to experience transformation, the pilgrim must become vulnerable—he must expand his edges, crossing borders into new and unfamiliar territory. When the pilgrim journeys to a place beyond what he calls "home," his senses are heightened, his vulnerabilities are brought to the surface, and his perceptions are tested. In allowing these different parts of himself to come to the surface, he is able to be fully present in his journey amidst the discomfort and uncertainty, the mystery and the beauty.

This sensation of crossing borders and becoming vulnerable is experienced in a literal way when traveling to unfamiliar cultures. Those encountered in these new and foreign territories might speak a different language, practice a seemingly strange religion, or eat food that the traveler has never tasted (or even *seen*) before. When presented with these differences, the traveler has a choice: to become fearful and reserved—refusing to try to speak the other language, consider the new religion, or taste the different food—*or* to immerse himself in the culture, embracing the challenges that arrive and opening himself up to new experiences. In fact, it is this distinctive and vulnerable way in which the traveler engages with the foreign way of life that makes him no longer a tourist, but a *pilgrim*.

As a traveler, the pilgrim is exposed to many cultures. But he will have the most valuable and transformational experiences when he is fully present with the things that might be unfamiliar, engaging with and learning from the culture in which he is traveling. It is often this very engagement with a new and unique culture that makes pilgrimage a Sacred experience.

When the pilgrim practices being open to the differences that surround him within another culture, he is also receptive to the new things he is discovering about himself, as well as the Divine. This not only impacts the pilgrim's journey abroad—it also informs how he encounters his own culture and how he engages the differences present within himself and his experience of God when he returns home.

For the pilgrim at home, the reverse is also true: by immersing himself in his own culture, he is prepared to practice awareness and engage with new cultures when he journeys beyond his borders. The pilgrim at home practices this by being active in the culture of his own community and by being aware of and celebrating the uniqueness it has to offer, both today and throughout history. With this intention, something beautiful happens: whether at home or abroad, the pilgrim who immerses himself in culture becomes a part of a greater story.

This week we'll explore what it means to immerse ourselves in culture by talking about what engaging customs, beliefs, location, food, and language means to the pilgrim both at home and abroad.

REFLECTION

Where do you experience vulnerability when immersed in different cultures? What are some new ways that you can immerse yourself in culture at home?

week four: day two

CUSTOMS

IN THE FIRST PILGRIM PRINCIPLE, when we talked about how the pilgrim looks for the Sacred in the quotidian, we explored creating rituals and the difference between ritual and tradition. A ritual, we said, is "a repetitive behavior" often practiced for the purpose of observance, while a tradition is "something that is handed down ... from generation to generation."

In this case, traditions are not so different from customs. In fact, the terms are often used interchangeably. But I find making a distinction between the two helps us to better name and understand different attributes of a culture, including our own. That's why when I use the word tradition, I'm talking about the grander practices of a culture, while customs are practices that are a part of everyday life.

If traditions refer to the bigger aspects of a culture like cultural history and celebrations, we might not always encounter them when traveling, depending on the time of year. If we do, perhaps it's because as tourists we've paid to experience some of the culture's traditions, like a Hawaiian luau or a gondola ride in Venice. But while the luau and the gondola are an important part of those respective cultures' history and tradition—trademarks, really—I can practically guarantee you that Hawaiians aren't always throwing feasts complete with hula dancers and Venetians aren't riding gondolas as a primary means of transport.

What they *are* doing is dressing far more casually and wearing sandals to work in Hawaii and eating late into the night in Venice, their meals always accompanied by a glass of wine. It can be fun and informative to discover a culture's traditions. But if tradition is the backbone of a culture, customs are the heartbeat. Customs can tell us more about the way of life of a culture, and knowing them and honoring them can help us truly experience that culture.

Guided Meditation

Like last week's guided meditation, our meditation today is a reflective one. In order to honor the customs of another culture, it's important to know our own customs, too. The pilgrim is aware of the difference between his customs and those of the culture which he is visiting and therefore doesn't let his own customs get in the way of experiencing and honoring those of another. For example, when she's in Istanbul, the Australian Christian covers her head when entering a Mosque, and when he's in England, the American coffee drinker gives tea with milk a try.

Grab your journal and settle in, closing your eyes and spending a few moments reflecting on your own customs, whether cultural or personal.

pause, reflecting on your own customs

Now write down the customs that came to mind. These are the practices that shape your way of living. They are unique and should be celebrated! They are also customs that you might need to set aside in order to honor and experience those of another culture. Being aware of your own customs and keeping this list in mind will help you do so.

The customs of other cultures have many things to offer us as well, even at home. For example, consider the value in the simplicity of Eastern spiritual practices for the Western world, which is often fueled by consumerism and achievement. Close your eyes once more and reflect on some customs from another culture that you think would enhance your daily life. After a few moments of reflection, write down these customs, too.

pause, meditating on customs from other cultures

In closing, I leave you with one of my favorite customs from yoga. At the end of a yoga practice or meditation, the teacher traditionally closes by saying *namaste*, with those practicing repeating it back. It essentially means, "The Divine in me recognizes the Divine in you."

And so, *namaste*.

PRACTICE

As you continue your week, find time to explore and incorporate these new customs, and notice any customs of your own that pop up that weren't on your list.

REFLECTION

How does it feel to name and celebrate the customs that you already have? How can you begin to celebrate other cultures by incorporating some of their customs into your daily life as well?

week four: day three

BELIEFS

BELIEF SYSTEMS ARE an important element of culture, and in many cases, it is by convictions and opinions that people in many cultures both define and differentiate themselves. The beliefs of a particular culture contain the culture's moral standards, its values, and especially its faith. They impact both our way of living and our way of seeing, which is why understanding the beliefs of another culture is especially important for the pilgrim wanting to be immersed.

Equally important for the pilgrim is understanding her own beliefs. If we don't know our own beliefs well enough—both their significance and their source—then we will be limited in how fully we can be immersed in another culture, because we will only be experiencing it through our particular lens. However, like customs, the pilgrim who understands her own beliefs and how they differ from others can set them aside temporarily as she seeks to become immersed in a new culture, eager to understand and know more.

Historically, imposing one's own beliefs on another has been a common practice. Whether it was the spreading of an empire or of a message, many unique cultures throughout the world have been lost, forgotten, or marginalized because a group of people more powerful came, enforcing their own beliefs.

Certainly there is nothing wrong with sharing your beliefs with others. What is misguided, though, is assuming that their beliefs have nothing to offer you. This is particularly true when it comes to matters of faith. Spirituality is something that is central to many, which means that it is intimate and something we hold close to our hearts and our identities alike. However, this also means that we often see things exclusively through our own experience of God, informed by our own culture and language, as we encounter new and different ways of spirituality.

Our experiences are both valid and valuable to our lives, for sure. But the truth is that many people in different cultures have their own experience of God informed by their own culture and language as well. By assuming that they do not bring something of equal validity and value, you not only miss the opportunity to understand them—you also miss the opportunity to learn from them.

Of course, there will be many beliefs, morals, and values of a culture that we might never agree with. But by seeking to understand the beliefs of another culture, we are better able to understand and more likely to learn from that culture. And it is when we understand and learn from another culture that we are truly immersed in it. *This* is the work—the *modus operandi*—of the fourth Pilgrim Principle.

PRACTICE

Practice engaging beliefs that are different than yours at home by visiting another religious community or reading about a culture with different traditions and belief systems. Enter this experience with an open mind, eager to understand and learn. You might end up finding God in places you never would have expected.

REFLECTION

What are some beliefs you have that might keep you from experiencing another culture? What are ways you can honor and learn more about the beliefs of others, whether while traveling or in your own community?

week four: day four

LOCATION

LOCATION IS PROBABLY the first thing you think about when encountering a different culture. When we talk about location, we can mean many things, particularly region, geography, or climate. Each greatly influences culture, its impact seen through a culture's lifestyle, cuisine, economy, and even worldview. As pilgrims traveling to new places on our search for the Sacred, location is often the first threshold we cross when immersing ourselves in another culture. It all begins when we set foot on dry land.

Aside from often being necessary to fully experience and immerse oneself in another culture, I describe location as the threshold of immersion because location is also indicative of something very important to the pilgrim: *presence*. Being present is necessary for immersion and allows the pilgrim to go deeper within the culture, surrendering to all that it has to offer.

In the same way, the location of our homes serves as the threshold of immersion in our daily lives and surrounding culture. The pilgrim who intends to be fully present when encountering new cultures abroad must first be fully present at home. However, this doesn't mean simply within the confines of the four walls of a house or the comfort found amongst friends, family, and community. These are important, yes, but they do not challenge us to engage things beyond our own worlds. This is why the pilgrim who intends to explore the world, immersing himself in new cultures, must first engage with the culture outside his front door.

This might sound simple, but for many it is not. We live in a world addicted to comfort, which often translates into many things that leave us anything but present and engaged with our location. We attend churches where people are like us, choose to live in neighborhoods where people are like us, and are even willing to pay more money so our children can attend schools with people like us. If we stay within the confines of the world we've so carefully created, we might live a comfortable life, but the only challenge we'll encounter will be "keeping up with the Joneses." And without challenges, we are not stimulated, we cannot grow, and we don't create meaning. Without the presence of difference in our lives, we cannot truly be pilgrims.

The pilgrim who seeks to be present in his location and cross the threshold of immersion while at home must intentionally engage difference in his daily life. Just as one travels beyond the borders of home to journey to a new location, the pilgrim must journey beyond the borders of his own comforts and seek to be present with, delight in, and learn from those whose way of living is different than his own. It is at this location where the journey of immersion truly begins.

PRACTICE

Start engaging difference at home by stepping out of your comfort zone and doing things differently. If you usually buy your books at a bookstore or online, visit the library and borrow some instead. There is always a diverse group of people at public libraries, and I have a feeling they aren't all bookworms.

Here's another idea: Rather than driving to work each day, commit to ride the bus for a week. You'll likely come across people who live in your neighborhood that you've never seen before. You could also walk somewhere that you would normally drive to. You'll be surprised by the new things you discover in your community when you're moving more slowly, and there will be plenty of strangers to greet along the way. The options are endless as long as you are looking for new ways to encounter people you might not otherwise within the comforts of your daily life.

REFLECTION

What is something you can do today to be present in your location beyond your home, family, and community?

week four: day five

FOOD

THIS PAST SEASON I spent one morning a week harvesting herbs and vegetables at an urban farm down the street from my house. Though I grew up in the Midwest—an area of the United States known for its agriculture—I had surprisingly little knowledge of how the food I ate was grown, let alone where it came from. And yet, food is an integral part of every culture, both what is grown in the region as well as what is served at the table.

The pilgrim who immerses herself in the food of the region in which she is traveling can learn far more about the culture than the tourist visiting museums or signature attractions. Food is a necessity in everyone's life, and when we seek to meet this common need, we come to the table desiring one thing: nourishment. When the pilgrim chooses to immerse herself in the food culture of a certain region, the pilgrim and the locals share a common table. Though language and customs might serve as barriers between them, they find nourishment together.

You simply cannot fully immerse yourself in a culture without experiencing its food. Whether sampling new and interesting produce while mingling with the locals at a city street market or stumbling through a foreign language while trying to order a signature dish at an endearing hole-in-the-wall restaurant, the pilgrim who pursues the food of a region learns a significant part of that culture.

PRACTICE

You can immerse yourself in the food culture where you live, too. Here are four ways to learn more about the food in your region and support the food culture in your area:

- *Shop at local farmers' markets.* Farmers' markets are popping up everywhere and are a great way to participate in your local food culture. By buying your produce at a farmers' market, you are immersing yourself in culture in three ways: you are buying food that has been grown locally, is in season, and you have the added benefit of buying your produce directly from the farmer.
- *Eat at local restaurants.* Local restaurants come in all shapes, sizes, and styles, but they all have something in common: they are owned by locals and created for the community. Eating at local restaurants not only supports the local economy—it helps maintain the local culture. What would be unique about a place if the only restaurants around were chains that could be found anywhere? (Remember this when traveling, too, and choose the unique experience!)
- *Participate in a CSA.* By participating in Community Shared Agriculture (CSA), you can immerse yourself in the local food culture in similar ways to buying your produce at a farmers' market, but there's one added benefit: since you pay for a share of a farm by the season, you partner with farmers through your investment.
- *Learn to cook the main dish of your region.* Different cultures have different styles of cooking—some like everything fried

up, while other cultures cook hearty stews with a unique blend of spices, always served over rice. Learning to cook the cuisine of your region can give you great insight into your culture, including the agriculture, the climate, and the spirit of the people. Go further by asking someone who was born and bred in your community to teach you how to cook the dish. I'm sure they have a recipe which they are very passionate and particular about. Who knows? It might have even been passed down for generations.

REFLECTION

What are ways that you can immerse yourself in your own culture by celebrating and supporting both the food created there and the people that bring it to you?

week four: day six

LANGUAGE

THE FINAL CATEGORY we're going to explore that the pilgrim encounters as she enters another culture is language. Language covers a whole world of difference, including not only foreign tongues, but regional dialects and popular expressions as well.

If you speak English, you are lucky enough to be able to navigate your way through most of the world with your mother tongue (or second, third, or fourth language—if that's the case, you can just skip right on ahead!). But there is a downside to this as well: since it is not often necessary for native English speakers to learn another language, many do not. However, learning another culture's language—at least enough to engage in some form of conversation—is important for the pilgrim seeking immersion.

This is even true for various dialects of the same language. There are many different dialects within the English language, but the ones I've most often encountered are American English (my own dialect) and British English. Some of these differences you learn the hard way, but once you know them, you feel far more engaged in the culture you are visiting.

While studying abroad in England, I visited a friend and his family in Birmingham. My friend and I were lounging late one after-noon, a cup of tea in my hand, when my friend's father came in and said, "Lacy, would you like some tea?" I responded by saying, "Oh, I already have some, thank you," thinking that it was kind for him to offer. However, that was not quite the case. My friend jumped in, translating what his father was really asking in his thick West Midlands accent: "What he means is, would you like some supper?"

"Oh!" I replied. After all these years of watching British TV shows and movies and reading British books, I thought that the British were simply having tea *all the time* (which really wouldn't be an over-statement). However, now that I know they also use "tea" to describe supper, I assume that many of those instances involved a little more than a hot drink and biscuits (not your flaky Southern biscuits, by the way, but that's another differentiation entirely).

Beyond tongues and dialects, language can be unique to a culture through expressions. At the graduate school I attended, The Seattle School of Theology and Psychology, it was common knowledge that because we were studying and processing things together, we shared a common language—always talking about story, self-care, "sitting with" things, and moving from "binaries" to the reality of "both/and."

Feeling a little foreign? That makes sense. I'm sure someone who glanced at this book without understanding the language we've been using might feel a little foreign, too. That's because even when we're talking about pilgrimage, we're using a particular language—*depar-ture, arrival, return, journey, path, longing, desire, Sacred, Divine*—these aren't words that many people use every day (see the glossary on page 9 if you need a refresher). But as you've been immersed in this language over the past many weeks, you'd probably say that you know more about what it means to be a pilgrim. It's amazing how deep language goes, isn't it? Whether it is the language of a country as large as Russia, the dialect of a neighboring region, or the common expressions used by pilgrims near and far, by learning new languages, we can truly know more of a culture and become immersed.

PRACTICE

This week, begin exploring your own language—the unique words or phrases that are common to you—and discover what story your language is telling. You can also begin paying attention to the language of those around you, particularly those who might be different than you, seeking to understand them in a new way.

And why not begin preparing for your next journey abroad by starting to study the language of a place you've always wanted to visit? It might seem daunting to learn it all, but "hello," "please," and "thank you" are good places to start.

REFLECTION

Do you have experience speaking different languages? What does it feel like when you begin to understand another language, whether new expressions, different dialects, or a new language entirely?

week four: day seven

GO FURTHER...

THIS WEEK I'VE OFFERED many suggestions for beginning to immerse yourself in culture—ways that will help you more fully experience the culture that surrounds you both at home and abroad. Here are more opportunities to immerse yourself in the customs, beliefs, location, food, and language of your own culture or another culture right at home:

Customs: Learn the customs of a culture where you'd like to travel

If you are traveling to a different culture soon, or simply have another culture that you'd like to visit on your bucket list, prepare for your journey by learning more about the customs of that culture. Tipping is an obvious custom that varies from place to place. Some customs even impact how you prepare for your journey, such as the clothing you plan to wear. Knowing customs like these not only help you blend in and show respect to the people you are visiting—they tell you more about the beliefs of the culture as well.

Beliefs: Share your new discoveries with another

As you visit religious communities or read about cultures with different beliefs, share what you're learning with friends and family and invite them to join you. By sharing your experiences of engaging difference, you can speak truthfully against any prejudices, and by expressing openness to things unfamiliar, you can encourage others to do the same.

Location: Learn the history of your hometown

We don't always have to go elsewhere to find good stories—there are probably many interesting things written within the history of your own community that have made it what it is today. By learning the history of your community, you can discover new things about your own story as well. If your family has lived in your hometown for generations, find out what brought them there in the first place!

Food: Cook a meal using only locally sourced ingredients

It might be challenging, but it will encourage you to discover more about what your own community has to offer, as well as connect you to the land and its Creator by prompting you to eat seasonally.

Language: Begin to learn another language spoken in your community

The world continues to be more and more of a melting pot, and you can easily find different languages spoken in large cities and small towns alike. Of course, those whose first language is not commonly spoken in their community can often remain at the margins. Show them they are a part of the community too by seeking to learn some of their language. You can even invite them to be conversation partners, regularly meeting to learn one another's languages. No doubt you'll learn many other cultural things, too!

REFLECTION

What are some ways you've begun to practice the fourth Pilgrim Principle in your life this past week? How has this impacted your spirituality and daily journey?

week five

A PILGRIM CREATES DAILY RHYTHMS TO GROUND HIMSELF

week five: day one

INTRODUCTION

THIS WEEK WE'RE EXPLORING daily rhythms, something I'm sure you're probably already participating in by reading this book. The fifth Pilgrim Principle highlights disciplines and characteristics of the pilgrim that we've already been talking about over the past four weeks, including spiritual practices, awareness, and intentionality. These things also help root us, despite what the day—or the journey—might bring. In fact, it's often the case that we feel most grounded when we engage in a daily spiritual rhythm and routine.

What does it mean to be *grounded*, and why is this important for the pilgrim? You might hear someone using this term when describing another person's character—a person who is grounded is authentic, dependable, or has a "good head on his shoulders." These are great qualities for sure, but when I think of the grounded pilgrim, I think of someone who is rooted and centered—someone who has a solid foundation offering stability, particularly in the midst of chaos and uncertainty.

Recently I read someone's description of a tree and why it is such a powerful image to them. She didn't describe the tree's leaves or its size, which is what we usually notice at first glance, but instead its deep and extensive roots. Though unseen, the root system is vital to the tree, establishing it and sending it nourishment. And as the roots grow deeper, firmly establishing the tree in the ground, the limbs grow wider and taller, expanding into the sky. Being above ground, the limbs are exposed to the elements, at times even shaken violently by the wind. Despite this, the tree remains in place, all because it is grounded.

If we are walking the road to Santiago de Compostela or simply walking to the bus stop on our daily commute, we are all pilgrims on a journey. And whether we want to admit it our not, chaos can show itself on each road we travel, always uninvited and often throwing us off course. The pilgrim knows, however, that it is only through facing these trials and laboring through the chaos that transformation can take place and new life can be born. And so, in order to remain rooted through the journey's challenges, like the roots of the tree, the pilgrim establishes daily rhythms to remain grounded.

One valuable way for the pilgrim to root himself is by establishing a daily rhythm centered on awareness and spiritual practices. The pilgrim who creates a daily rhythm commits time each day for regular and deepening spiritual engagement—a rhythm which, like the nourishment of water for the tree, creates stability and facilitates growth. The pilgrim also knows the importance of cultivating time each day for self-care, searching within himself to determine his present physical, spiritual, and emotional needs and committing to honor them.

When the violent winds in life threaten the pilgrim's path, the pilgrim has deep roots that he can depend on because of his daily rhythms. In the midst of challenges, these daily rhythms in the pilgrim's life help to ground the pilgrim, calling him back to awareness and intention. This week we'll explore what it means to have a daily rhythm in body, mind, soul, spirit, and presence, nourishing our roots and finding ways to help them grow deeply.

REFLECTION

Do you have any daily rhythms? What are the things in your life that help you feel grounded in times of chaos?

week five: day two

BODY

WHEN WE EXPLORED the second Pilgrim Principle, "A pilgrim practices somatic spirituality," we talked about how important the body is to our spirituality and how it can be used as a vessel for Sacred Encounter, inviting us to engage our spirituality in new ways. In the same way, the pilgrim knows that the exterior physical journey is a conduit to the interior spiritual journey. As we seek to ground ourselves, centering the body plays an especially important role.

Though it's not often recognized in Western medicine, the wellness of the body is connected to the wellness of the mind or soul. Think about it: When you're angry, does your body tense up? When you're nervous, does your heart pound quickly? When you're anxious, do you find that you might not be breathing as often or as deeply as you should?

No wonder we have expressions such as "Don't forget to breathe" or "I have butterflies in my stomach." Our bodies respond to the emotions and thoughts we're experiencing, whether we're aware of it or not. Sometimes our bodies can tell us that something is wrong when we don't even know it—they hold our struggle and anxiety when we are unable or unwilling to do so otherwise.

Just as discomfort in our bodies can remind us to check in with our thoughts or emotions, when we experience heavy or complex thoughts and emotions, centering our body can help us to center our mind and soul. In this meditation we're going to go through an exercise that you can use on your own in the future when you want to center your body in order to help center your mind, soul, and spirit, calling you back to presence.

Guided Meditation

Get into a comfortable seated position with your feet on the floor. Close your eyes, gently breathing in and out for a few moments, slowing your breath, slowing your body, slowing your mind.

Now we're going to begin a breathing exercise used in yoga and meditation, called *ujjayi* breath (pronounced oo-jai-ee). *Ujjayi* breath brings relaxation to the body, cultivating deep breathing that takes us all the way to our edges, where our lungs are fully empty and then conversely where they are completely full. To ensure that your stomach and lungs are expanding when you breathe, it might be helpful to place one hand on your chest and the other on your stomach.

Slowly breathe in through the nose, filling first your belly, then your chest, until your lungs are completely full. Pause, holding the breath in, and then slowly breathe out through your mouth with a slight "ha" sound (like waves in the ocean), releasing first your chest and then your belly, until your lungs are completely empty. Pause there, holding the breath out, and repeat. Your breathing will sound like waves rolling into the shore.

Closing your eyes, continue the *ujjayi* breath, breathing in to the count of four, pausing, and then breathing out to the count of four and pausing once more.

continue the breath for a few minutes with your eyes closed

Begin to relax your breath into a normal and steady pace. You might find that your body is starting to feel centered already. Now we're going to practice awareness of our bodies, beginning with our toes all the way to the top of our head. This practice helps your mind to stay focused on your body and can also help you recognize where you're feeling pain or tension that you might not have noticed otherwise. It is also a good practice when you want to call yourself back to the present moment.

read each prompt one-by-one below,
following the instructions slowly as you go along,
taking time to pause and notice how you feel
between each prompt

- Begin with your toes and the soles of your feet firmly on the ground. Without moving, feel the energy in your feet—the warmth, your blood flowing, the feeling of them touching the ground.
- Now slowly move your focus up to your knees. How do they feel?
- Continue moving up to your hips, feeling the energy of your body against your chair, grounded and rooted in your current position.
- Now move your attention up to your chest. How's your breathing? Feel your chest rise and fall with the steadiness of your breath, and notice how it moves your entire upper body.
- Shift your focus outward, down your arms and into your resting hands. Do you feel the energy flowing, even though they're not moving? Remember with gratitude all of the work your hands do each day.
- Now shift your focus back up your arms to your shoulders. This is a place where many people hold a lot of tension. Make sure your shoulders are back, opening your chest, and imagine breathing into that space, caring for and relieving any tension

that's there.

- Finally, move up to your mouth, your nose, your ears, your eyes, until you've reached the top of your head. Breathe clarity and peace into a place that's so often consumed with thoughts.

bring your meditation to a close
by returning to the ujjayi *breath*

As you come to an end, close your eyes once more and sit in stillness for a few moments, noticing how you feel.

PRACTICE

Do this meditation on your own anytime you feel chaotic and need re-centering, remembering how physically feeling grounded can lead to emotional, mental, and spiritual centering.

REFLECTION

How does your body feel after this meditation? How do you feel? In what ways can you incorporate exercises like these in moments when you need to feel grounded?

week five: day three

MIND

As a PILGRIM, you might find that your body, soul, and spirit commit to the journey far more easily than your mind does. Of all of the parts of ourselves that often need re-centering, the mind can be the most challenging. At least that is definitely true of my own experience. Sometimes the part of our minds that just can't seem to stop running is referred to as the "monkey mind," and it seems to be great friends with the Inner Critic as well—that voice inside that always appears to know where we're lacking. Many days it can be difficult to sift through all of the noise to what we know to be true and real.

There are multiple practices that are used to quiet the mind, giving rest from our racing thoughts and returning us to the truth. Meditation is an especially useful daily rhythm to ground the mind and can be practiced alone with the intention of clearing the mind or can be guided, as we've been doing at the beginning of each week.

Another regular rhythm that allows us to re-center the mind is praying the hours, an ancient tradition often practiced in liturgical settings and by religious orders, such as the Benedictine tradition. When reading through the *Rule of St. Benedict* a few years ago, I was surprised to discover that members of the order were even required to rise at midnight to pray! (Thankfully, I recently learned that rising in the middle of the night was a far more common and natural occurrence before artificial light was used, so perhaps Benedict should be posthumously awarding bonus points for those who do it now.)

I first learned about praying the hours while studying at The Seattle School of Theology and Psychology. At The Seattle School, a bell chimes each day at the hours of nine, noon, and three. Each time the bell chimed we were encouraged to pause—even if we were climbing up the stairs or in the middle of a sentence—and be reminded of God's presence, whether through prayer, silence, or some other form.

In religious orders and some liturgical traditions, when the hour of prayer strikes, passages are read, psalms are sung, and prayers are recited. Following a common liturgy can be a powerful practice, knowing that many others around the world are joining you in your intention. Whatever is done when the bell rings and the time of prayer is at hand, the purpose is the same: to remind us of the presence of the Divine and to call us to return to what we know to be true.

PRACTICE

When you are easily carried away with the distractions of the day, praying the hours can help ground your mind, interrupting the chaos in order to return you to your Sacred intention as an everyday pilgrim. A modern way to do this is by setting a repeating alarm on your computer or your phone. Choose a few times a day to pause from your activities when the alarm goes off and say a prayer or spend a moment in silence. You can also recite a mantra that is meaningful to you—a phrase that helps you return to yourself in the midst of chaos, reminding you of your true self and the presence of the Divine. If you'd like to be more traditional in your praying of the hours, try *The Book of Common Prayer* or research *The Rule of St. Benedict*.

REFLECTION

What is a word, phrase, or prayer you can use to help center your mind when you become anxious or distracted?

week five: day four

SOUL

WHEN I WAS IN SEATTLE a few months ago, walking along a familiar sidewalk I'd walked on many times, I noticed something that I hadn't seen before. While the cement was drying, someone had written the following prophetic phrase in the ground: "Don't lose your soul." Though a simple message, I was compelled to pause and literally breathe it in, wanting to absorb it fully. As I walked mindlessly between point A and point B, it served as a powerful reminder, because in our everyday lives it is so easy to become lost.

The soul serves as the pilgrim's compass. It is the place where questions become quests—where intuition is birthed and longings explored. The pilgrim who has lost her soul has lost her way. In order to not lose her soul, the pilgrim must meticulously care for the very tool that helps her navigate. And to care for the soul is, in effect, to care for the self.

Like many practices of the pilgrim, self-care can often seem counter-cultural. In a world that has a myriad of ways of saying "get over it," there is little patience, respect, and understanding for taking the time to care for the self. In fact, we're so used to hearing these stigmas that when we do take the time and space to care for ourselves, we are often plagued with guilt for seeming selfish or not being productive.

But in reality, self-care is just the opposite. Taking time to care for the self allows us to more fully care for others. It can also help us be more productive in other areas of our lives because when we regularly practice self-care, tending to our needs and our areas of deficit, we can be more fully present to the task at hand. Just as a compass tells a traveler her direction, self-care serves as a touchstone, helping us to realign with our true selves in a world that can often be bumpy and chaotic.

In order to practice pilgrimage every day, it's important to establish daily rhythms of self-care. Routinely checking in with ourselves and offering care and space where needed helps us to remain in touch with our souls and thus aware of and intentional in our own journeys. What you do to care for the self will always serve as fuel for life's pilgrimage.

PRACTICE

Find ways that you can regularly practice self-care each day. This could look different from person to person, depending on your needs and circumstances. Since replenishing energy is a vital form of self-care, a great way to start learning how to best care for yourself is by determining if you are extroverted or introverted. Extroverts get energy by spending time with others, while introverts need to recharge by spending time alone. Once you determine which fits you and your needs best, make sure to carve out some quality time with others or alone each day to refuel.

You can also practice self-care by investing in the self—body, mind, and spirit—and by being kind to yourself, especially when difficult feelings like fear or self-doubt arise. Though difficult, these feelings are valuable because they help you to locate your self and your soul.

REFLECTION

Do you have rhythms of self-care? What are some things you can begin to do daily to better care for yourself?

week five: day five

SPIRIT

I GREW UP AROUND the morning ritual of daily devotions, except that I would often do them at night, reading along with tired eyes, prayers floating into the abyss as I drifted off to sleep (God still accepts half-said prayers from the abyss, right?). School started early and I was always so tired when I woke that I don't think I ever even considered having my quiet time in the morning.

I finally discovered the blessing of the morning ritual when I was prone to wake up early, had lots of time on my hands, and had easy access to a hammock while in Uganda. After graduating from college, I spent nearly six months in Uganda with a gap year team from the United Kingdom. We lived in rural Uganda and worked primarily creating children's programs for the surrounding schools and churches.

The anti-malarial medication I was taking affected my sleep, so each morning I found myself rising much earlier than the rest of my team. One morning, early on in our time there, I crept out of our house with my travel hammock that I had brought all the way from the US for a moment such as this and strung it between two trees. Lying there—early morning snacks stuffed in the hammock's pocket, tea perched on a nearby stoop, Bible and book in hand—I realized I had stumbled upon my Sacred space.

Each morning I continued to wake up earlier than the rest of my team, even without an alarm, as if my new Sacred space was beckoning me out of bed. My morning ritual consisted of reading, praying, and simply being. It was an introvert's heaven and became something I very much depended upon to thrive.

When we explored the first Pilgrim Principle, "A pilgrim looks for the sacred in the quotidian," we learned about rituals, defining them as a way of enacting meaning. Through returning daily to my Sacred space and participating in my morning ritual, I was enacting meaning, both in the moment and for my day and journey ahead.

Remembering how my practice in Uganda impacted my spirituality and left me feeling rooted, as I returned home I was determined to find new Sacred spaces and create new morning rituals. Over the years my morning ritual has morphed and changed. It has been left behind and started up again with new perspective, but it has always remained a treasured time, one that has been valuable for my spiritual well-being.

Daily spiritual practices and morning rituals are important for the pilgrim as well. The practice of pilgrimage is all about enacting meaning, and to stay on the Path, each day must begin with returning to the pilgrim's Sacred intention. As a pilgrim on a journey right at home, you can be reminded of your quest by returning to your Sacred intention through your own morning ritual.

PRACTICE

Here are a few steps to help you start a morning ritual of your own:

- *Find a time.* Does it feel best to begin your morning ritual right after you wake up? Or perhaps once you're ready for the day or while you're eating breakfast would be more suitable. Choose whatever feels most spacious for you. As you consider a time, also think about the length of time you want to spend doing your morning ritual. This might determine what you do.

- *Find a place.* Morning rituals are often personal, so the best location is probably one that is private. A good place might be a chair by a window or maybe outside on a porch swing. Wherever it may be, make sure it is somewhere where you are able to connect with the Divine, making it a Sacred space.

- *Determine your spiritual practice(s).* It could be as simple as pouring a cup of coffee and reading through a devotional book. Perhaps you spend your time in centering prayer or meditation (more on these tomorrow), practicing yoga, journaling, creating, or reading poetry. Simply choose a practice that helps you connect to the Divine and enables you to feel like your true self, whether the practice is traditional or unique to you. Do one or many, or perhaps consider changing them monthly or seasonally. Trying out new spiritual practices is a great way to stretch your edges and grow your faith—something the pilgrim knows well.

REFLECTION

What would your ideal morning ritual be? If you already have one, what does it look like, and how does it set the tone for your day?

week five: day six
PRESENCE

FOR THE PILGRIM, Sacred Encounter doesn't occur in the past or in the future—it happens in the only place time truly exists: *the present moment*. In order to open himself up to Sacred Encounter, then, the pilgrim must be fully present. Just as we've explored different ways to become centered in body, mind, soul, and spirit, it is equally important for the pilgrim to establish rhythms of practicing presence (we talked about this previously when we reflected over our relationship with time and explored immersing ourselves in a location).

One of the most significant ways to practice presence is through centering prayer, because presence is the only requirement of this ancient way of encountering the Divine. Sometimes referred to as contemplative prayer or even simply meditation, the intention of centering prayer is this: to be present with your truest self and the Divine.

Like meditation, centering prayer is a specific amount of time during which you quiet your mind and rest in God's presence. By doing this, you create space for the Inner Witness, the communion of the Holy Spirit and the true self (so important to the pilgrim that the seventh principle is devoted to it). In a world where we are constantly bombarded with words, both without and within, centering prayer is a difficult practice. However, it is also a forgiving one that in reality requires of us little: simply our consent and the willingness and faith to continue to create space when we face distractions. All you need is a place to sit, a set time, and a "Sacred word" to help you return to your intention: communion between your truest self and the Divine.

PRACTICE

Today, try practicing centering prayer. Here's how to begin:

- *Start in a seated position,* either on a chair with your feet rooted to the floor or cross-legged on the floor. To ensure good posture, which is essential for comfort and focus, make sure your hips are higher than your knees (you can do this easily by sitting on a pillow).

- *Set a time for your desired length of prayer.* If you're new to meditation, you can start with five minutes, but traditionally centering prayer is practiced for twenty minutes at a time, twice a day. However, this is only tradition and shouldn't keep you from practicing. You certainly don't have to do it twice a day, but I encourage you to go out on a limb and give the twenty minutes a try. You'll survive even if it's your first time, I promise. Yes, your mind will inevitably wander during this time (mine always does), but what matters is that, despite your many wanderings and returns, you continue the practice for your chosen amount of time. Set a timer so you're not tempted to peek!

- *Chose a Sacred word or phrase* that reflects your intention. You will use this word to help you return to stillness when your mind becomes distracted. I use the words "peace" and "presence." You could also use a phrase, such as "Lord, hear my prayer," or "Here I am." There's no formula to choosing a Sacred word—simply choose a word or phrase that is meaning-ful to you and significant to your intention and offering. This will be your Sacred word each time you practice.

- *Begin your practice.* If you'd like, you can ease into the practice by reading a poem or psalm or by breathing in and out fully and deeply. After a few rounds of breathing you might repeat your Sacred word to yourself silently. Then let your mind settle into the presence of the Divine. I find it's easiest to create space by literally imagining a clearing in my mind—a space of Sacred communion where thoughts and memories might dance on the outside, but aren't allowed to enter.

- *Continue to return to God's presence.* It's likely that you'll regularly be distracted by the thoughts vying for your attention in your peripherals, and that's okay. It's all a part of the process. When this happens, I find the following helps me to leave my thoughts behind and return to my original intention: become aware of the distraction, label it accordingly (thinking, rehashing, planning, etc.), dismiss it back to your periphery, and refocus on your mind's clearing and your offering by repeating your Sacred word a few times. Someone once told me to not feel guilty about the number of times I am distracted during this practice, but rather to be encouraged by the number of times I return, since returning is a great exercise of faith (and an appropriate practice for the pilgrim, no doubt).

- *End your time.* When your timer goes off, be gentle. Slowly awaken your senses to the world around you, and close your time with the Lord's Prayer, another poem or psalm, or a few final deep breaths.

REFLECTION

What was your experience with centering prayer like? Were you able to be kind to yourself when distractions arose? How are you feeling after your experience?

week five: day seven

GO FURTHER...

A COUPLE OF DAYS ago we talked about morning rituals. Perhaps you already have one and are looking for new practices to try. Or maybe you're just developing your morning ritual but are not sure what practices to begin with. We have already explored many spiritual practices that you can use in your morning ritual throughout this book. Here are a few more ideas for morning rituals involving body, mind, soul, spirit, and the practice of presence:

Body: Exercise regularly

This is advice you hear a lot, but I'm sure you never thought you'd read it in a book about practicing pilgrimage at home. However, in addition to the obvious health benefits, consistent rhythms of exercise remind us that our body is also a significant player in our well-being, and it needs our regular attention to be at its best. It's also well-known that moving our bodies is a great way to get out of our heads, and I have a feeling that's something each of us could use daily.

Mind: Participate in daily readings

Returning to a text each day not only has a profoundly centering effect—it can also inspire growth over time. You can go the traditional route by using the daily scripture readings in *The Common Book of Prayer* or reading through a devotional guide, or you can read a chapter each day in an inspirational book or a new poem by a mystical poet. I suggest 14th century mystic Hafiz or the late poet, author, and priest John O'Donohue (quoted by Christine Valters Paintner in the foreword).

Soul: Establish a rhythm of Sabbath

Sabbath is traditionally a weekly rhythm when you set aside your work one day a week (this even means to-do lists!) for rest, delight, and awe. Thanks to Saint Irenaeus, we know this to be true: "The glory of God is man fully alive." Practicing rhythms of Sabbath helps us to return to our true selves and to the Divine on a regular basis. You can practice a daily Sabbath during your morning ritual by setting aside an hour of your day where rest, delight, and awe reign supreme. No doubt we could all use that!

Spirit: Write your own psalms

One of the things I love about the various psalms in the Bible is that they are a confession and exploration of a myriad of emotions in the presence of God. It is an amazing example of how we can fully bring ourselves to the Divine and a great reminder of how in the end, everything is a spiritual matter. When you feel spiritually distant or uprooted, try seeking the Divine through writing your own psalms of exploration and confession, letting your questions and desires flow freely. It would be especially interesting to see the variation in psalms written over a particular season in life.

Presence: Keep a journal

With daily tasks and to-dos to distract us, it's so easy to go through our days without ever having to be fully present with ourselves and with God. Regularly writing in a journal is a great way to press pause and go deep within, being present to the thoughts and emotions swirling around inside and the movement of the Sacred Guide in our lives.

REFLECTION

What are some ways you've begun to practice the fifth Pilgrim Principle in your life this past week? How has this impacted your spirituality and daily journey?

week six

A PILGRIM CARRIES HERSELF
WITH CURIOSITY

week six: day one

INTRODUCTION

CURIOSITY IS VITAL for the pilgrim on a journey. In fact, it's built into the fabric of her being. At her core, the pilgrim is a seeker, and although it might not seem like it at first, there is a difference between seeking information for knowledge—a common, one-dimensional quest—and seeking it in order to guide one's life. The difference is that the seeker who wants knowledge is on a quest to collect information, while the seeker who searches for guidance is fueled by her curiosity.

Today, curiosity is something often only associated with children (and even then it is sometimes discouraged). Many of us have forgotten how to be curious and have consequently stopped growing, for growth and transformation are fueled by curiosity. However, even Jesus himself encourages curiosity in his followers in the Sermon on the Mount: "Ask and it will be given to you; seek and you will find; knock and the door will be opened to you."[6]

Though this verse might sometimes be interpreted as Jesus saying he will provide for our needs, interpreting it as welcoming curiosity takes its meaning far deeper and makes its possibilities seemingly endless:

Why do we ask? *Because we are curious.*

Why do we seek? *Because we are curious.*

And why do we knock? *Because we want something behind that door.* (Also, we're very polite.)

Through this interpretation, Jesus is essentially saying: "Ask and you will be given answers to things you never would have known otherwise; seek and you will find me in unexpected places; knock and you will be welcomed into a world of wonder and possibility." Asking, seeking, knocking—*this* is the work and the blessing of a curious pilgrim. And this is required at each stage of the journey—the *departure*, the *arrival*, and the *return*.

Even prior to physically leaving, the departure stage begins with the pilgrim's curiosity: she *asks* by locating her place of yearning, she *seeks* by naming her desires, and she *knocks* by taking action, initiating her pilgrimage.

The journey itself is filled with many points of arrival and Sacred Encounter. But the pilgrim will not be aware of, or benefit from, these moments without curiosity. To practice awareness along the journey, the pilgrim *asks* by remembering her quest. She *seeks* the Sacred by intentionally engaging each moment and encounter. And she *knocks*—extracts meaning from the Sacred Encounters—by naming them.

Even in the stage of return, it is the pilgrim's curiosity that helps to bring the journey to a transformative end. In *asking*, the pilgrim reflects on all aspects of her journey—both where she endured trials and where she saw glimpses of the Divine. In *seeking*, the pilgrim finds meaning in these encounters. And in *knocking*, the pilgrim crosses a new threshold, carrying into the future the lessons and experiences of her recent quest.

This week we'll explore five expressions of fostering curiosity—openness, willingness, desire, delight, and perspective—beginning to ask, seek, and knock ourselves.

REFLECTION

Is curiosity welcome in your life? In what areas has your curiosity been stifled? If there has been space for curiosity in your life, where has it taken you?

week six: day two

OPENNESS

To EVEN BEGIN carrying himself with curiosity, the pilgrim must have a stance of openness. In order to be curious, the pilgrim must be open to new possibilities and perspectives, open to asking new questions, open to naming desire, and open to the presence of the unknown. Needless to say, maintaining a stance of openness is not an easy task—like many other characteristics of the pilgrim, it requires daily practice.

Guided Meditation

In this meditation, you'll start at square one by setting the intention of openness through using your body. As you learned in the meditation for the fifth Pilgrim Principle, the condition of your body is connected to the condition of your mind, soul, spirit, and presence. With this exercise, you're opening the body and breathing into that open space. It will also help you recognize what it physically feels like when you are being open and curious versus when you are closed off.

This exercise is a common practice in yoga, where opening and breathing into the chest is said to open the heart, opening us up in all areas of life. If yoga is new to you, simply view this as a ritual—an enacting of sorts. We act on the desire to be open in all areas of life by beginning with the body, calling forth openness in other areas of our lives through our intention. The act of opening the body then becomes a prayer and a model for our desire, something we can return to when we feel ourselves closing off.

Start in a seated position, either on a chair with your feet rooted to the floor or cross-legged on the floor. Sitting up straight, place your hands on your knees and let your arms relax (you'll need to find a way to prop this book open in front of you). With your hands firmly on your knees, pull your upper body forward, your elbows hugging your side, your shoulders back, and your chest sticking out like a pigeon. Breathe in deeply, filling that space.

Now, with your hands still firmly on your knees, push your upper body back, straightening your arms, tucking your chin into your chest, and curving your back. Breathe out.

Continue this cycle, pulling yourself forward, opening your chest and breathing in, and then pushing yourself back, straightening your arms, curving your back, tucking in and breathing out. Once you find that you're in a rhythm, close your eyes to remove any external distractions.

continue this movement for a few moments with your eyes closed

As you continue this exercise, opening your chest and breathing in and then curving your back, tucking in and breathing out, invite specific areas of your life in which you want to be more open into the practice. As you pull forward, opening up, bring to mind the area in which you need to be more open. It might be the beliefs or opinions of others, a change that's occurring in your life, or a new perspective. Breathe into that space, opening up your chest and your heart and setting your intention. As you push back and breathe out, release whatever hinders you from being open in that situation.

Continue this cycle for a few more minutes, and as new areas come to mind, open yourself up to them as well. If nothing comes to mind, simply continue the exercise, breathing in deeply and opening yourself up to what is to come.

continue the movement, bringing to mind
areas that require more openness

As you come to a close, slowly return to stillness, sitting up straight and finding a steady breath. With your eyes closed, bring to mind once again the areas in which you need to practice openness. Take in a final deep breath and let out a deep sigh, ending your meditation and releasing all opinions, judgments, and things of the ego that keep you from being open.

PRACTICE

When you notice that you are feeling closed off to something in your day, whether in a conversation with a friend or loved one or even while watching something on the news, pay attention to your body language. If it is closed off, see if opening up your body, such as uncrossing your arms or sitting up straight, can help you feel more receptive and open in the moment.

REFLECTION

In what ways do you feel more open after this meditation? How do you think practicing openness will change the way you respond to times of uncertainty or conflict?

week six: day three

WILLINGNESS

IN SPIRITUALITY, having questions has long been associated with doubt. And doubt, in a world that relies upon knowledge and certainty, is seen as confusion and weakness. With faith, we're often told that doubt is a time for testing, filled with temptation, and that could be so. But the curious pilgrim views his doubts and questions differently.

In fact, he does not see his doubts and questions as signs of confusion and weakness that lead into the abyss. He's not even too concerned with finding the answer. That's because the question says enough in itself. But in order to ask bold questions and search further for deeper meaning, one thing must be present in the pilgrim: *willingness*. Even without yet knowing the answers, the questions birthed out of our willingness can tell us many things. They can tell us what we long for, what we're missing, what we love, and what we'd like to understand.

Take, for example, the age-old question: "What is the meaning of life?" (No small feat, eh?) If the pilgrim with this question is simply looking for *the* answer, then he might never find it. I have a feeling there are *many* answers, varying from generation to generation, religion to religion, and person to person. The pilgrim could learn more of himself, and perhaps also of God, by more closely examining his question.

While the answer might not be clear, the message within the question is pretty straightforward. Look closely—the longing is indicated right in the question. By asking what the meaning of life is, the pilgrim is expressing his desire for meaning and significance. Whether asked in curiosity around the table or as a cry from a pit of despair, the presence of the longing for meaning remains the same. It is an essential question, present within all of humanity throughout history.

How do you tend to a longing for meaning? You actively seek meaning. For the pilgrim, the question indicates the journey at hand. The journey for the pilgrim asking about the meaning of life becomes a journey in search of meaning. And by setting out on an intentional journey, the pilgrim is certain to find meaning, for he is making meaning simply by committing to the journey.

PRACTICE

What are your questions, and what can they tell you of your longing, and consequently, your quest? Take time to list a few of the questions that are present in your life. They might be more general questions, or they might be unique to you. Either way, they will tell you of your longing if you look closely. As questions come to mind, write them down and then take some time to examine them—not looking for an answer, but rather, your *quest*.

REFLECTION

Based on the questions that you have, what do you think your quest might be? When questions continue to arise throughout your day, consider what the quest might be behind them. Even if it's ordinary, it's still enlightening.

week six: day four

DESIRE

Desire has gotten a bad rap. When we think of desire we think of selfishness and the deep coveting of something we don't have. At other times we think of something scandalous, making desire seemingly taboo. Few people associate desire with curiosity. But curiosity is desire's playground, and when we open ourselves up to the curiosity of desire, a journey is born. However, in order to become in touch with desire and determine where our journey begins, we must first reclaim desire as good and familiarize ourselves with what desire looks like in our souls and how it manifests itself in the everyday.

What makes desire ultimately good? Our deep desires are conduits to the soul, indicating to us the state of our well-being. But in order to read them and act on them, curiosity must be present. To see beyond the stereotypes of desire, past the material desires of the false self to the rich desires of the soul, you must ask one of the central questions of the pilgrim: *What do I long for?*

When you ask this question, the answers might flow rapidly: *I long for freedom and autonomy. I long for space to create. I long for community. I long for purpose.* Each of these represent valuable and pressing desires, signified by how quickly they arise. But these desires have deep roots, and by carrying herself with curiosity, the pilgrim can go much deeper to the root of these desires, uncovering the uninhibited longings of the soul.

When the pilgrim does this, she might find that a longing for freedom and autonomy becomes a desire for escape from a sense of oppression. The desire for space to create is at its roots a longing for self expression. A longing for community is more deeply a longing for connection. And the desire for a sense of purpose is exposed as a primal longing for a sense of worth.

Our desires can also be masked behind everyday circumstances, requiring curiosity in order to be uncovered. Buried behind moments of frustration or disappointment are deep longings of the soul. The presence of fear exposes desires for certainty and affirmation, and feelings of boredom or restlessness hide the essential human longing for meaning. Even moments of delight can tell you of your desires, because delight is desire's celebration, a longing fulfilled.

It is through this work of curiosity and of uncovering and naming desire that the pilgrim's work begins. It is our desire that forms our questions, and as we know already, the questions are what form the quest. Further down the Path of the Pilgrim, it is the curiosity of desire that awakens us to our intuition, and as we will soon learn, it is intuition that guides us along the way. At the end of the journey, it is through curiosity that our desire is fed and reborn, sending us home with a new journey and a richer, more embodied path.

PRACTICE

When you notice negative feelings within yourself today, such as frustration, disappointment, depression, or boredom, consider them an opportunity to practice curiosity and wonder about what unmet desire is hidden behind your emotion.

REFLECTION

What do some of your desires tell you about your deeper longings?

week six: day five

DELIGHT

It's SUMMER NOW, and my husband and I are two months into our first vegetable garden. This year we planted purple bell peppers, jalapeños, cucumbers, wax beans, and three varieties of tomatoes. Ever since we planted our garden in May, I have been fascinated by the growing process of food that I've eaten for years, but apparently never fully understood. As a result, tending to the garden has been a great source of delight.

At least once each day (and often more), I venture out to the garden, checking in on the plants, as if we're good friends. I love discovering blooms, knowing now that they are a harbinger of new fruit, and I routinely stare in awe at my vining cucumbers, amazed that yet another tendril has spiraled around a string since I've been away. "It's like it's alive!" I exclaim, not able to hide my excitement from anyone who asks about the garden. "I mean, I know it's alive, but it's *alive* alive!"

Yes, it seems that keeping a vegetable garden has brought me so much delight that I have lost my ability to articulate it clearly and can only describe my wonder with child-like excitement. It was no surprise, then, when I came to realize that by growing a garden I have not only been cultivating food—I have also been cultivating my curiosity through the gift of delight.

As we've discovered this week, curiosity is a natural trait of the pilgrim, for without curiosity, the journey would never begin. But for those who have forgotten how to be curious, it's hard to know where to start. Often, to cultivate curiosity in our own lives, we need external inspiration. In order to carry ourselves with curiosity, it must be cultivated, and the best place to start is in the places where we find delight, for it's there that our curiosity lies waiting for our embrace.

The pilgrim knows this and doesn't wait until she reaches another country or a life-altering circumstance to ask questions or be filled with awe—she nourishes her curiosity at home, relishing in her delights. And when she allows herself to delight, celebrating her curiosity, she begins to become curious in other areas of life as well—she begins to carry herself with curiosity.

Tomorrow we'll explore another way to do just that, but for me, gardening is a good place to start. As I've been writing, it seems a tomato that's long been green has begun to ripen into an orangey-red by the warmth of the sun, and I have to go outside and look at it. What can I say? I'm curious.

PRACTICE

To begin exploring what brings you delight, collect images of things that attract your attention and put them in a place you see on a regular basis, such as on your refrigerator, on a bulletin board in your office, or as a slide show screen saver. After a while, you might begin to notice some themes and will be able to go even further in your search for delight. For example, if most of your pictures are of delectable desserts, take a baking class, and if your inspiration board is filled with images of the quaint English countryside, plant a garden that has its own way of transporting you there.

REFLECTION

What are the things that make you curious and bring you delight? How can you incorporate these things into your everyday?

week six: day six
PERSPECTIVE

"THAT'S ART?" my college friend asked. I was showing him some pictures from my freshman year spring break trip to Chicago, where we had spent an afternoon at the Art Institute of Chicago. The photo was of an installation piece—a string of illuminated lights sprawled across the ground in the corner of the room. I took the picture simply for the purpose of showing him—I knew this would be his reaction.

Being an art student, I heard comments like these frequently from similar friends studying business or the like. I myself was studying graphic design, which is more of a practical art, requiring the perfect combination of right brain creativity and left brain analytics. Stuck in the middle, I didn't always understand the meaning behind such abstract installation pieces, but I wasn't ready to claim that they weren't art, either. As far as I could see it, I had two options: ignore it because I didn't understand it, or become curious.

So what is art, really? Here's how the dictionary defines it: "the quality, production, expression, or realm, according to aesthetic principles, of what is beautiful, appealing, or of more than ordinary significance."[7] What is beautiful? What's appealing? What has significance? Is there a common standard—a yardstick by which to measure all of this so we can know, once and for all, what is art?

Not really. What is considered beautiful, appealing, and significant is all based on perspective, which means it can be different for different people. However, there's a common thread within the dictionary's definition of art that can help us make sense of it all—things that are perceived as beautiful, appealing, and significant have one thing in common, despite differing opinions—they are all seen as *meaningful*.

There are many things we call art—music, dance, sculpture, poetry. Some people might consider stacking stones an art, while others might feel their art comes into being as they stand in front of a stove. No matter the medium, art is ultimately about creating meaning, and in order to appreciate the art of others and uncover meaning in their work, we must often show curiosity, seeking to understand the piece from the artist's perspective.

For the pilgrim, curiosity and perspective go hand in hand. When on a journey, practicing curiosity allows the pilgrim to see things from new perspectives, and trying to see things from different perspectives helps the pilgrim to be more curious. The endless world of art offers a great way to exercise both curiosity and perspective at home. It also provides an opportunity to engage the pilgrim's greatest task and search—making and finding meaning.

PRACTICE

Practice making meaning by creating your own art, whether it's on a canvas, in a song, or through an arrangement of flowers. It doesn't have to be like other things you've seen or heard—remember, it's all about perspective, and you know what is meaningful to you.

REFLECTION

How is it to create and not critique yourself? What new perspective do you have about your creativity and how you find meaning?

week six: day seven

GO FURTHER

CARRYING YOURSELF WITH curiosity can be difficult to relearn, but by continually returning to your intention to be open and willing, making room for desire and delight, and practicing viewing things from different perspectives, you can cultivate the curiosity needed to send the pilgrim within you journeying out into the world. Here are five more ways to help you begin to carry yourself with curiosity through openness, willingness, desire, delight, and perspective:

Openness: Have a conversation with
someone whose views differ from yours

It sounds hard, and it probably will be. But I have a feeling that you have someone in your life with whom you don't necessarily see eye to eye on a particular issue (at least I hope you do, but that's another conversation entirely). Hearing others out when you don't entirely agree with them is a great way to practice openness, since it's far easier to remain closed off. A healthy conversation with someone you might disagree with signals to the ego that your way isn't necessarily *the* way, which will also prepare you for the many similarly dissonant encounters in your journey. Would there even be a journey if our way was always the way and we were never challenged to be open to something beyond ourselves?

Willingness: Begin your search

Remember some of those questions you wrote down? Now dig deeper by finding others who are asking the same questions and searching for something more. Start conversations with people you trust, and explore new territory through books or blogs on the subject. You might just be inspired to write a bit about it yourself!

Desire: Write your desires down

Naming our desires helps us to be curious about ourselves and what our lives could be. Make a list of the 10 things you desire out of life. You might end up being surprised by what comes out. Who knows? This list might have a way of reshaping your priorities, your circumstances, and your life's journey.

Delight: Add delight into your day

Decide on a time frame each day that you will devote to something you delight in, and stick to it. Taking time to delight each day will broaden your curiosities, because where there's delight, there's wonder, and wonder is contagious—it will start to spill into every area of your life. You could also add something to your home or office that you delight in, such as a painting, a photo from a vacation, or a plant. Whatever it is, it can serve as a constant reminder of what you love and what you long for.

Perspective: Visit an art museum

Hopefully you've taken the time to start creating your own art and making meaning or intend to do so. Doing this will help you understand first hand what it's like to infuse meaning into your own creation. Then take some time to visit an art museum, and pay special attention to the things that might make you think, "huh?" Practice exploring different perspectives by searching for meaning within the piece. What you find may not be at all what the artist intended. Still, the exploration allows you to see things differently; it evokes something within you, which is the hope of every artist.

REFLECTION

What are some ways you've begun to practice the sixth Pilgrim Principle in your life this past week? How has this impacted your spirituality and daily journey?

week seven

A PILGRIM SEEKS TO KNOW
HIS INNER WITNESS

week seven: day one

INTRODUCTION

TODAY WE ENTER the final week in this *Pilgrim Principles* journey. And though the journey is coming to a close, in a way we are ending with a beginning, for it is by practicing the seventh Pilgrim Principle that we start any journey, even this one. This also means that you have been practicing the seventh Pilgrim Principle throughout these past seven weeks. In fact, it is this principle that led you here. The seventh Pilgrim Principle calls us to deeper awareness of ourselves, of God, and of the place where the two intersect. It is from this place that questions are first whispered, beauty is first glimpsed, and meaning is first realized. This place is the *Inner Witness*, and it is the focus of the seventh Pilgrim Principle.

While you certainly have come to new awarenesses in this journey, the term *Inner Witness* might be new for you. The Inner Witness is a phrase commonly used by spiritual directors to refer to the true self that dwells within us. The Inner Witness is that place of interior retreat and rootedness—the place of both the indwelling of the Holy Spirit and the true self—and is precisely what inspires our search for the Divine.

This is the common search of all humanity, and yet many do not know their Inner Witness—their truest self and their source of connection to the Sacred. From the pain and brokenness that inevitably accompany life, they have come to believe God is not real. Or perhaps they have been told that God is real—and even believe it—but they do not truly know God, because they are told that the Image of God within humanity only existed at the time of creation, not that it is something that we all bear and have access to each day.

One religious denomination that recognizes the imprint of the image of God on humanity is the Eastern Orthodox tradition of Christianity. According to the Eastern Orthodox doctrine known as *theosis*, the purpose of life is the uncovering of the image of God—or *imago Dei*—within each one of us. It is a lifelong journey into the likeness of Christ, who is both fully human and fully Divine.

A good way to describe this is by the metaphor of polishing silver. Like magnificent silver, the image of God is embedded within each one of us, though it has been tarnished by the pain and brokenness within the world. The journey to uncover the image of God within us is like polishing the tarnished silver, and with each intentional movement we reveal more of our true selves as image bearers, and more of the Divine, whose image we bear.

No matter the journey, this is the essence of the pilgrim's quest. Led by the Sacred Guide, the pilgrim who seeks to know his Inner Witness journeys toward his true essence as an image bearer and consequently also the Divine. This week you'll discover how you can better seek to know your Inner Witness through acceptance, awareness, intuition, insight, and finally, enthusiasm.

REFLECTION

What practices are already a part of your daily life that help you to better know your Inner Witness—the image of the Divine within and your true self?

week seven: day two

ACCEPTANCE

THE PATH OF AWAKENING begins with acceptance, something that is necessary with the practice of each principle. In the process of awakening, the pilgrim learns to accept whatever the ordinary day brings. She starts to accept her body as a source of wisdom and blessing. She begins to accept the resources available to her and her responsibility to use them as tools to communicate love and meaning. Through immersion, she accepts the cultures around her, both her own and of the other. She accepts her daily needs and takes the time to meet them. Finally, she accepts her questions and begins to delight in her curiosities. But what is most important is that she begins to accept herself.

As you have gone through *Pilgrim Principles*, you have been on a journey of awakening. You have honored your longing to make meaning and your search for something more. And it's my hope that you've learned much along the way. Of course, it's easy to turn these discoveries and insights into a list of things to start doing, attain, or reach for. I do hope that these daily readings have expanded your edges, bringing you new opportunities and perspectives. But if we start to view them as items on a to-do list, we can easily become bogged down.

Instead, I hope that as pilgrims we can begin seeking to know our own Inner Witness by fully accepting ourselves as we are, struggles and all. For if we truly believe that the Inner Witness is the place where the Divine and the true self meet, then at our essence we are already whole; our journey is to simply return to that essence. This journey begins with acceptance.

Guided Meditation

Acceptance of the self requires acceptance of the very things that we try to resist. In this final meditation, we're going to practice acceptance through giving ourselves grace—something that, though we give it to others, we don't often offer ourselves. We'll do this by going through our days, moment by moment, accepting our feelings, actions, and our very selves as we go along.

Find a comfortable and quiet place. Close your eyes and take a few moments to center yourself, perhaps through one of the exercises we explored with the fifth Pilgrim Principle, such as steady breathing or saying a mantra or prayer.

pause, closing your eyes and centering yourself for a few moments

If you're reading this in the morning, you can go over your day yesterday; if you're reading this in the evening, try reviewing today. Starting at the beginning of your day, bring to mind feelings or circumstances that left you unsettled, frustrated, saddened, or ashamed that you have not yet accepted.

Behind each of these moments is a vulnerable self longing for love and acceptance. Offer these things to that vulnerable place within with a nod of affirmation that says, "I see you," or perhaps some encouraging words toward yourself, such as "It's okay," or, "It makes sense that you feel that way." If it was an action that was unkind, such as blaming someone else, you can still offer yourself acceptance in that moment without affirming the action by noticing the deeper desire within—for example, "Oh, that happened again; some part of me must still be afraid."

With each moment of acceptance take a deep breath in and out, releasing the negative feeling into the past and moving on to the next moment.

spend a few moments reflecting on the rest of your day
in turn, offering yourself acceptance

As the day you are tracing comes to a close, return to a steady breath and take a few minutes to savor this acceptance of yourself, almost as if you were absorbing it into your body and soul. In this moment filled with acceptance, you are fully connected to your true self and your Inner Witness. In closing, take a final deep breath in and out, taking this glimpse with you as you leave this time.

PRACTICE

You can take this exercise further by looking back on your life as well, going through it as a timeline and offering your past self grace in the situations where you did not receive acceptance, either from others or yourself. This practice might bring up memories that are hard to bear, but it can also offer deep healing, rewriting your past to impact your future journey.

REFLECTION

What did it feel like to reflect back on difficult moments and offer yourself grace? As you accept yourself in these moments, do you feel any closer to your true self and your Inner Witness?

week seven: day three

AWARENESS

As I CONTINUE TO explore the practice of pilgrimage, I keep coming back to two main characteristics that seem to be pillars of the pilgrim: *intention* and *awareness* (you've probably already picked up on these common themes throughout this book). Practicing each of the Pilgrim Principles requires intention and awareness, and it is because of both that you find yourself on this journey. Awareness is especially vital for the pilgrim, because it is awareness that leads her to her search—awareness of her question, awareness of her desire, awareness of the existence of something more. If anything in this book has resonated with you, then your journey toward awareness has already begun. You are in the process of awakening, and your quest awaits.

Undoubtedly, this awakening is largely a journey toward self-awareness. When we better know ourselves, we are also more tuned into the world that surrounds us. There are many ways to begin the journey of self-awareness, and this book is full of suggestions. In fact, each practice in this book is in part a practice of awareness, and so your journey has already begun.

You can also invest in your journey toward awareness by regularly meeting with a professional, such as a therapist or a spiritual director.

Therapists and spiritual directors can serve as guides for the journey, and they are honored to be witnesses of this process within you. Their presence will also help to keep you accountable, urging you to continually return to your quest.

It is important to remember that the journey toward awareness can lead to wholeness, yes—but it is also difficult journey. In the process we not only become more aware of the goodness within and without, but also of darkness, sadness, anger—things that are often hard to bear. The pilgrim is no stranger to this stage of the journey. Like a wise guide, a therapist or spiritual director will be able to support you during these times, holding onto the hope of your search for you when the road is difficult. These guides know the hard truth of the journey toward awareness: the only way past the darkness is through it.

PRACTICE

One way you can learn more about yourself right now is by discovering your personality type. Becoming aware of whether you're introverted or extroverted can completely change the way you interact with others as well as yourself (we talked about introversion and extroversion earlier when exploring self-care). As a pilgrim, knowing your personality type can also tell you more about what type of journey might be most meaningful to you. With the Myers Briggs typology assessment you can discover whether you're an introvert or extrovert, how you gather information (through sensing or intuition), how you make decisions (through thinking or feeling), and how the world appears to you (based on judging or perceiving). Find out your Myers Briggs typology and what that means about you by taking a free assessment online.

The Enneagram is another typology tool that is valuable for self-awareness. In my own experience, it has taught me more of myself than any other typology assessment because of its holistic nature.

In addition to naming your personality type, the Enneagram also says what a healthy and unhealthy version of your type looks like and highlights what your virtues and vices might be. It reveals both what you fear and desire the most, and it can no doubt make you more aware of your essence. Find out your Enneagram number and see if it resonates with you by taking a free assessment online.

As you continue to learn more about yourself, remember that the above suggestions, especially when it comes to typology, aren't textbook—they're only tools. Your Inner Witness is your true guide on the journey toward awareness, and it's my hope that these tools can help you along the way.

REFLECTION

What has helped you become more self-aware in your life? This can include relationships, circumstances, and even tools like typology assessments.

week seven: day four

INTUITION

OFTEN REGARDED AS the sixth sense, intuition is natural and essential, yet so elusive and mysterious. But then again, the Inner Witness can be as well. If our journeys are led by the rumblings and desires of the Inner Witness, then it's our intuition that guides us to the places of Sacred Encounter.

When people talk about following their intuition, they often use phrases like, "I *felt* that it was true," "I had a *sense* that it would turn out that way," or "I can't explain it, I just *know* it." Intuition is a deep knowing, but often unlike the world's definition of knowing. Typically intuition's message can't be outlined neatly with facts or figures or even expressed in words. It is a knowing deep within our hearts and in our bones—a message stemming from our subconscious, our true selves, our Inner Witness. Some might say it is a message from God.

Being able to tap into and reap wisdom from our intuition can be beneficial in many ways. It can guide us in decision making and let us know where we stand. It can warn us of what lies ahead or tell us what action to take in the present moment. It can also be an indicator of the state of our relationship with our essential self. For example, many of us are plagued with bouts of self-doubt from time to time. When we pause to explore these feelings, our intuition can serve as a spotlight, shining light into the darkness, speaking truth into the chasm that has separated us from our true selves and our inherent worthiness.

For the pilgrim, intuition is like a lantern for the journey—a light in the darkness, indicating to the pilgrim his next step and guiding him along the path. When he holds it closely, he too will be in the light. And if he is separated from it, he can always find it again if he searches for the truth. So how can the pilgrim pick up this lantern at home? How can you bask in its light and search for its truth within the darkness? How do you begin to recognize and use this sixth sense in everyday life?

Like many practices of the pilgrim, it starts with awareness. Intuition often appears as a sharp and sudden feeling or a deeply-seated yet indescribable certainty. When you have these experiences, pay attention. What are they telling you? If it is indeed a message from the Inner Witness—a glimmer of light in the darkness—then it will be a message that moves you in the direction of truth, life, and love. If this is the case, then the next step in following your intuition is to take a risk—a step of faith by the light of your intuition, even when the path ahead is still dark with uncertainty.

I could say more, but it would be of no use, for our intuitions are each as unique as our true selves and our Inner Witnesses, and so your intuitive path lies in your hands only. To begin to follow it is an act of intuition within itself. What comes next is up to you.

PRACTICE

When you notice that you have a certain feeling about a particular decision or situation, but you can't necessarily explain it, pick up your lantern and look closely to see what your intuition might be trying to reveal. It can be risky to act on things based on a feeling, so as you determine what steps to take and which voice to follow, remember this: the Inner Witness—the intuitive whisperer—is always wanting to lead you toward life and your true self.

REFLECTION

Do you feel in touch with your intuition? If so, what happens when you act on your intuition? If not, what are some ways you might begin to explore and act on your intuition each day?

week seven: day five

INSIGHT

We can often learn more of the essence of something through a little insight. This can come from others, from history, or from our very own experience. Insight helps us to read the current circumstances and to take informed action. The pilgrim uses insight to determine her quest, along the journey through times of trial and challenge, and also upon return when applying lessons learned from the pilgrimage to her daily life.

When seeking to know more of our Inner Witness—our very essence—there are many things that can serve as guides, offering insight. As I've mentioned before, spiritual direction and psychotherapy are great tools in drawing out our true selves in ways we could not do on our own. Books that introduce new ideas and spiritual practices that give us new and unique experiences also provide great insight.

But it's likely that your Inner Witness—the very thing which of you seek to know more—is trying to offer insight, too. One of the most common ways that the Inner Witness tries to communicate with us is through dreams. People often don't want to give much credit to the power and truth held within our own dreams. Their significance, however, is even woven into the narratives of Scripture.

In the Bible, dreams were often the place where the Divine communicated powerful messages to humanity—a practice true to the role of the Inner Witness, the place where the Divine and our true selves meet. In psychology, dreams are seen as expressions of our psyche, a part of ourselves that carries knowledge both known and unknown. As the psyche's playground, the dream world is often filled with repressed thoughts and feelings that, for some reason or another, we don't allow to surface. As pilgrims, we might see it as the Inner Witness trying to break through, showing us the truth we often hide from but which, paradoxically, can ultimately set us free.

Of course, just as there are many schools of psychology, there are also many theories on dreams. One of the greatest and most studied advocates of dreamwork is the late psychotherapist Carl Jung. Jung believed that dreams serve as a window to the unconscious and that dream analysis offers valuable insight into the parts of us that are unknown, guiding us toward wholeness, or as some might say, to our true selves. Paying attention to dreams can help the pilgrim connect to the Inner Witness in extraordinary and surprising ways. No wonder we use the word "dream" to refer to not only the state of our mind when we sleep, but also to the deep desires we hold in real life.

PRACTICE

To mine for the treasure held within your dreams and find out what your Inner Witness might be trying to tell you, start a dream journal. Place the journal by your bed, and each morning when you wake up (or in the middle of the night, if you had a particularly jarring dream), write down what you can remember of the dream. No need to analyze it just yet, unless the meaning seems obvious to you. Simply continue this practice for a few weeks or months.

After you have a fair number of dreams recorded, consider what patterns arrive. Are there figures that consistently appear in your dreams or themes that occur repeatedly? You might notice that some of your most troubling dreams occurred when you were going through a stressful time in life. Once you discover some themes or simply find things that stood out to you, do some research into what they might mean. Speak to a therapist or spiritual director who does dreamwork or try analyzing the dream on your own. When you stumble upon meaning, you'll know. It doesn't mean it will feel good, but if the insight is coming from your Inner Witness, you will get a sense of its truth.

REFLECTION

Have you had any dreams that have caught your attention and curiosity? What insight do you think they might be trying to offer?

week seven: day six

ENTHUSIASM

AFTER SEVEN WEEKS on this journey, it feels appropriate to end by exploring what got us here in the first place: *enthusiasm*. When you think of enthusiasm, you're probably thinking of excitement (which, of course, is a great thing). But did you know the word enthusiasm means so much more? Enter the etymological dictionary, the meaning-seeker's gold mine. Here's what it says:

Enthusiasm (n.)[8]
c.1600, from *entheos* "divinely inspired, possessed by a god," from *en* "in" + *theos* "god."[8]

"Divinely inspired"—does that not describe the pilgrim? And is it not true for you as well? Enthusiasm is a *spark*—a reaction to the meeting of the Divine and the true self—and it is the action of the Inner Witness. Enthusiasm literally translates as "in God." Is that not amazing? And it is this enthusiasm that fuels the pilgrim's quest— from departure, to arrival, to return, and back again.

You see, pilgrimage is not a single journey, but a lifestyle. It's a daily practice that keeps us engaged in our search for the Sacred, and it is through paying attention to the Inner Witness and kindling the flame of enthusiasm that we continue our search, especially in the everyday.

So, what are you enthusiastic about? Where is your spark? Where is your fire? Where do you meet God and come alive? Remembering each of the Pilgrim Principles, where do you experience God in the everyday, and how do your senses connect you to the Sacred? What resources can aid you on your search, and how will you come to better know God through the eyes of others? When do you feel rooted, and what makes you curious? What is your Inner Witness longing to ask, seek, and discover?

The place of your enthusiasm is where your journey is born. This is when excitement is no longer a great synonym for enthusiasm—although the journey is Sacred, it doesn't mean the task is easy and the road is trial free. If it were easy, everyone would be doing it. But that's not the case. As Jesus said, few will enter.[9] Few will recognize the spark of enthusiasm within. Few will acknowledge their search, and few will courageously enter into the unknown for the sake of that which they seek.

But as pilgrims, that is what we are called to do. And we know that it is worth it, because we recognize that spark and know it leads to something more—something *Sacred*.

PRACTICE

Begin to identify what makes you enthusiastic by noticing where you feel a spark of excitement, wonder, or curiosity. Once you feel a spark, act on it! Make a commitment to pursue it further, whether that means sitting down to write a poem, starting a new career, or setting out on a journey. Whatever the spark may be, when it comes from your Inner Witness, it will always lead to the Divine.

REFLECTION

Where is your spark? What are you *en-thus-iastic* about? Where will you begin your journey?

week seven: day seven

GO FURTHER...

HERE WE ARE at the end of the seventh week with a final opportunity to go further. I know these last seven weeks have been rich with new ideas, questions, and possibilities, but don't become too overwhelmed! These are only suggestions, and remember, the Path of the Pilgrim is a lifelong journey—not something to be mastered, let alone in seven weeks. Your journey has begun, and I hope you will continue to use this book as a tool along the way.

Here are some additional suggestions to help you seek to know your Inner Witness through acceptance, awareness, intuition, insight, and enthusiasm:

Acceptance: Practice saying "I accept..."
Not out loud, unless that's what works for you. When you notice you're trying to push down a feeling or are dwelling in shame from the past, say it to yourself as a mantra. When unacknowledged, it's easy to get caught in vicious cycles that never serve us or bring us closer to our Inner Witness. When this is happening to you, take a deep breath and simply say, "I accept that I cannot go any further," or "I accept that things turned out that way." It won't change every-

thing, but it's an important step in ceasing the cycles that distract us from our true selves.

Awareness: Recognize destructive thought patterns

Many of us can be easily distracted from our true selves through obsessive rehashing of a situation that didn't go the way we had hoped, getting caught up over others' opinions of us, and worrying about the future. These patterns can be so common that we don't even know when we've succumbed to them. However, you can gain power over them by naming them when they arise. Whether it's rehashing, worrying, or planning, naming these patterns as you begin to recognize them helps bring awareness, returning you to the present moment and reminding you that these distractions are only a negative downward spiral, taking you further away from your true self. Identifying these patterns will help you return to your intention.

Intuition: Pay attention to your feelings

A feeling is a response to something external or internal—something in our past, in our present, or what we think is yet to come. The feelings that you have—especially those that pop up suddenly or unexpectedly—can tell you something of your truth, whether it's revealing something you already know or drawing attention to a belief you have which is inauthentic. Begin to notice those sudden and unexpected feelings and start to wonder what truth your intuition might be trying to reveal.

Insight: Learn from a friend

Asking a friend or loved one who knows you well to give insight into your life is a great way to better understand others' experience of you and to know whether your Inner Witness is shining through. You can ask any question and go as deeply as you'd like, but here are some simple questions to start with: What are the three qualities that you feel make me stand out? Do you encounter the Sacred through some of my thoughts or actions? What do you think I'm passionate about?

Enthusiasm: Find others who share your enthusiasm

There is no better feeling than realizing you are not alone, particularly when it comes to the vulnerable places where we ask questions, seek answers, and fuel dreams. Begin sharing your enthusiasm with those around you whom you trust. It's my hope that in your sharing, you will find companions for the journey. Perhaps you will even light the fire for another pilgrim.

REFLECTION

What are some ways you've begun to practice the seventh Pilgrim Principle in your life this past week? How has this impacted your spirituality and daily journey?

BENEDICTION

LONG AGO WHEN pilgrimage was in its heyday, and when there were knights and new cathedrals and jousting matches and plagues, pilgrims setting out on their journeys gathered together with their families and their parish priests to set their affairs in order, say their goodbyes, and be blessed.

To bless someone is to speak words over their journey, and for you, Pilgrim, I want to do the same. The journey on which you're embarking is long and treacherous, and though you're not as likely to die by the sword or of the plague or freeze in the cold as did your 15th century kindred spirits, it's bound to be a struggle. Following the Path of the Pilgrim is like walking along a dirt trail and sometimes forging your own path while it seems everyone else is speeding along on the smooth asphalt of the freeway that you hear in the distance.

But those cooped up in their cars and in their lives will only see the beauty you encounter through a tinted window. They will only see the people you see through a barrier of protection. And the whispers of the Sacred? They won't be able to hear them through the noise of the radio top 40, drowning out the silence that can be so hard to face. They will get from point A to point B, sure—eventually we all do. But they won't be present for the journey, and that's where life, and the Divine, exist—in the here and now, in the meeting of hearts, in the conquering of dragons and the naming of desires—and especially in our everyday lives, engaged with intention.

This is what we've been exploring over these past seven weeks. And though your journey continues after you close this book, ours here is almost done. Consequently, this blessing is also a benediction—an "utterance of good wishes."[10] It is at once a sending and a commencement, echoing the words of many wise pilgrims before it—those who followed with conviction the road less traveled. The seven Pilgrim Principles are but guideposts along the Path of the Pilgrim. It's you who must choose if you will follow the way.

And so, blessings to you, Pilgrim—

May you continue to look for the Sacred in the quotidian,
Delighting in the presence of the Divine in things so ordinary.

May you continue to practice somatic spirituality,
Your senses taking you deeper on your Sacred journey.

May you continue to be a good steward of resources,
Blessed with wisdom, discernment, and above all, gratitude.

May you continue to immerse yourself in culture,
Investing in and learning from others both near and far.

May you continue to create daily rhythms to ground yourself,
Regularly returning to your true self and your Sacred intention.

May you continue to carry yourself with curiosity,
Asking questions, seeking meaning, and filling your days with delight.

And may you never cease to seek to know your Inner Witness,

BENEDICTION

That place of truth inside you and the indwelling of the Sacred Guide.

Go in peace to love, to serve, and to journey. Practice these Pilgrim Principles and the Path of the Pilgrim will be at your feet, both at home and abroad.

NOTES

Introduction
[1] Cousineau, Phil, *The Art of Pilgrimage: The Seeker's Guide to Making Travel Sacred* (San Francisco, CA: Conari Press, 1998), p. 82. This is a classic book on pilgrimage. When someone new to pilgrimage asks me for recommended resources, I send them here first.

Week One: Day One
[2] dictionary.com

Week One: Day Three
[3] Definition paraphrased from dictionary.com
[4] Definition paraphrased from thefreedictionary.com

Week Two: Day One
[5] dictionary.com

Week Six: Day One
[6] Matthew 7:7

Week Six: Day Six
[7] dictionary.com

Week Seven: Day Six
[8] Shortened description of word origin from etymonline.com
[9] Luke 13:23-24: "[23]Someone asked him, 'Lord, are only a few people going to be saved?' He said to them, [24]'Make every effort to enter through the narrow door, because many, I tell you, will try to enter and will not be able to.'"

Benediction
[10] dictionary.com

ACKNOWLEDGMENTS

I NEVER INTENDED to write a book—at least not now, anyway. I thought I was writing an online course, which perhaps was just the Trojan Horse I needed to get myself to sit down and write, finally putting these inklings of my heart and soul onto paper. What was birthed out of those countless hours of writing (and many more staring into the abyss) was this collection you hold in your hands, and I have many people to thank:

My parents, for giving me so many opportunities to travel when I was young, planting the seed of my love for travel early, and continuing to water it so that it could grow.

Those who shaped me at The Seattle School of Theology and Psychology, who in turn helped shape this book; with special thanks to Tom Cashman for his spiritual guidance (and for assigning the paper that caused me to determine my *Pilgrim Principles*!); Dr. Dwight Friesen for bearing witness to my work with pilgrimage and encouraging me in my intuition; and to Paul Steinke for his presence and voice in my life in many ways.

Kayce Hughlett, for affirming this spark within me from the beginning and giving me language to blaze a new path. Ronna Detrick, for her continued support, encouragement, guidance, and example.

Those who have connected with me along the way: Dana Reynolds, woman of wisdom, for your excitement and influence; and Mary DeJong, who, though we have never met, shares my heart for pilgrimage—I am eager to see how our journeys will align.

And of course, Christine Valters Paintner, who wrote the foreword for this book, and has gone before me and is always willing to answer any question that I have about my quest; I look forward to learning more about pilgrimage from her.

Linda Roller, for editing this book, and others who gave early feedback on the content and whose impressions can be felt in these pages: Abby Hollingsworth, Ryan Moore, Katie Jensen, and Hilary Ann Golden.

Victor Saad, for reviewing the book and being an entrepreneurial inspiration. Kelsey Kopecky and Lara Sink of *Feather & Belle*, for allowing me to use their music for the book trailer—it fuels the energy that I hope will in turn send readers out into their lives and the world as everyday pilgrims. Kristen Gilfillan for lending her beautiful handwriting to the book trailer at a moment's notice.

And Dan and Stacia Cumberland, my fellow Masterminds and friends, for not only offering feedback on my words but for also participating in the process, including brainstorming sessions, the creation of an amazing cover image and book trailer, and for being the first to say, "Lacy, this could be a book." With their valuable help, it now is.

And of course, my loving husband Kyle, who believes in me and what I have to offer the world sometimes more than even I do. He calls me toward my true self daily, which is to say that his presence in my journey is Sacred, indeed.

A SACRED JOURNEY

Founded and curated by Lacy Clark Ellman, author of Pilgrim Principles: Journeying with Intention in Everyday Life, *A Sacred Journey is a website devoted to spirituality and intention in travels and daily life and regularly features the personal stories of pilgrims. Learn more at asacredjourney.net.*

Made in the USA
Charleston, SC
10 January 2014